PRAISE FOR *PROPERTY FIT*

A comprehensive guide to property investment in Australia that is BS free. This book is a must for anyone looking to build wealth through property.

Paul Benson, CEO and founder Guidance Financial Advice, author and host of Financial Autonomy podcast

Whether you're buying your first home or an investment property, you need to have a good appreciation of the value of time and be willing to do the work. If you can do that, then Luke's book gives you the knowledge to execute the rest of your strategy.

Kate Campbell, How To Money

Property Fit is comprehensive, easy to understand and clearly and logically goes through each step that a property investor must consider before diving in.

Joanna, member of The Property Mentors

Property Fit is a good companion to *Let's Get Real*. It puts readers inside the experienced head of Luke Harris, a property investor and strategist who helps Australians with a passion for property get wise about how to achieve their goals.

Cindy, member of The Property Mentors

PROPERTY FIT

GET YOUR PROPERTY PORTFOLIO IN SHAPE FOR FINANCIAL FREEDOM

LUKE HARRIS

ABOUT THE AUTHOR

Luke Harris has an extraordinary depth and breadth of personal experience across business, property and investing covering more than two decades. His entrepreneurial mindset kick-started his property career early, and with nothing more than big dreams, persistence and a can-do attitude, Luke has learned some valuable lessons and obtained some enviable results.

Today, Luke continues to grow significant wealth through his personal portfolio and for his clients at The Property Mentors, a Melbourne-based agency that helps clients develop the skills, mindset and knowledge to grow their property portfolio. Luke's personal 'why' is to help members reach financial freedom through property so they can go on to successfully fulfil their own dreams and ambitions. He is the co-author of *Let's Get Real* (Major Street Publishing, 2018). *Property Fit* is his second book.

Published by Major Street Publishing Pty Ltd
PO Box 106, Highett, Vic. 3190
E: info@majorstreet.com.au W: majorstreet.com.au M: +61 421 707 983

A catalogue record for this book is available
from the National Library of Australia

NATIONAL
LIBRARY
OF AUSTRALIA

Printed book: 978-1-922611-16-1
Ebook: 978-1-922611-17-8

Cover design by Tess McCabe
Internal design by Production Works
Printed in Australia by Ovato, an Accredited ISO AS/NZS 14001:2004
Environmental Management System Printer.

10 9 8 7 6 5 4 3 2 1

CONTENTS

PREFACE

Ever since I was 20, I've been into property. I've always loved the thrill of searching for, finding and buying a property that I know will be a perfect fit for my portfolio. Back then, my ambitions were big. My dream was to swan around in a Lamborghini, sipping lattes all day. I wanted lots of properties, a $50 million portfolio, a superyacht, a Maserati – sure, why not? – and first-class travel. I thought that was the life of a property investor – cashed up and time rich.

Of course, it's no surprise I made plenty of mistakes. I can see now I spent many years muddling my way through investment after investment, learning and failing on repeat. I was simply investing for the moment, looking at one property at a time, one deal at a time, and then throwing around strategies left, right and centre in the blind hope that something would stick and I'd start making my millions. There wasn't much connecting of dots. It's a familiar story.

At the time, I didn't know any other way. I didn't have anyone in my corner: no friends, family or work peers who were experienced in investing, let alone anyone I knew smashing goals with excellent results. But clearly, what I was doing was not going to move me in the right direction.

I realised I was aiming for things that were completely unrealistic – the superficial wants of a naive 20-something-year-old with no life experience. I was making big decisions without looking at the long-term and figuring out the big plan and the right strategy – the right *property fit*.

So, after ten years of investing, at the age of 30, I forced myself to critically evaluate my life to self-assess what the hell I was doing. What did I want out of life? What would make me happy? Really happy, I mean.

I realised that what I thought I wanted wasn't actually what I wanted. Let me repeat this for you, because this is fundamental for every investor: *What I thought I wanted wasn't actually what I wanted.*

It was a bombshell moment for me. Suddenly, I could see it all laid out in front of me. What I wanted was a lot simpler than I'd thought: my own house to live in and a handful of investment properties providing me with enough income to give me the lifestyle that I wanted. This was achievable; a five-million-dollar income wasn't necessarily unachievable, but it wasn't what I needed to live the lifestyle I desired.

The revelation also kickstarted a fresh mindset. I'd gotten real about what I wanted out of life. I finally knew my 'why'. So, I decided to take a step back and take 18 months off, which gave me an opportunity to establish my work as a professional property investor and launch a sole-trader property consulting service. During this time, I pulled apart what works and what doesn't work for most property investors. It's not *that* difficult to buy property – so why aren't more people retiring wealthy from property? I wanted to know why and started putting systems and processes in place to help property investors get better results than from going it alone. From there, in 2014, I went on to establish The Property Mentors, helping to guide others on their own property investing journey with the right mindset, strategy and action plan to create an extraordinary life. Helping others is my other 'why'.

I guess my definition of 'rich' has dramatically changed over time, too, as I have grown up. The dream of having 'lots of money' in my teenage years is worlds apart from my current goal of building long-term, sustainable wealth. In 20-plus years though, you'd expect priorities to change.

Fast-forward another decade and I've hit 40. I've been there, done that – still doing it! – and lived to tell the tale, and I'm at a place now in my investing career where I'm very happy. Right now, I have a core bunch of properties in my portfolio that I'll keep, as well as a range of commercial properties and development sites around Australia. They'll continue to give me a six-figure income for the rest of my life. I have financial freedom, and I'm heading towards the next level with my portfolio. After all, successful long-term property investing is a journey, not a destination. You need patience, perseverance and an unwavering desire to reach your goals, for which you also need to be financially, educationally and emotionally fit. Plus, with investing, as with sport, there's always another level. As your education and experience increases, so should your results. But it's worth highlighting that building long-term sustainable wealth is not a sprint: it's a marathon, and the work always comes before the results.

As I write, Australia is rolling out its vaccination program, and the property market is back full throttle. Of course, we've just experienced one of the most unprecedented and challenging periods in our lifetimes with the COVID-19 pandemic, but we've been through other economic and financial shocks over the past 40 years.

During such uncertain times, I've been spending a lot more time talking to our members, and I've been attending more client meetings with my team. I wanted to get a hands-on feel for what's happening in the market and what clients want from advisors, to see if people were still muddling their way through decision after decision, just like I did when I was younger. Unsurprisingly, it turns out, they are, and every market shock only makes each decision harder and more complex.

All of this has paved the way for the book that you're holding now. It made me ask myself, 'How can I teach people to find the right *property fit* for their portfolio, so they can succeed instead of failing? How can I show them how to put together the right pieces of their property puzzle, with the right strategy, so they can find greater success over the long term, starting with the end in mind?'

If this all sounds attractive, let me bring it home for you. Australia is one of the luckiest countries in the world. We have low interest rates, excellent long-term property growth, population growth, a free health system, a stable government and, perhaps most incredibly, the privilege of being able to buy whatever and wherever we want. When people refer to Australia as 'the lucky country', I truly believe that's because we have the most fantastic opportunities here. I've travelled all over the world, and every time I return home I'm grateful to be living in Australia at this moment in history.

This investment landscape creates incredible opportunities, all available today. I strongly believe that there is no better time to invest in Australia than right now, which you'll learn more about as you read the book. After all, buying property should be an enjoyable journey. Tread carefully, think strategically and read on, so that you too can achieve your own version of success with the right property fit for you – whatever that may be!

INTRODUCTION

A big welcome to *Property Fit*. This book picks up where my last book – *Let's Get Real* – finished. Just like any fitness plan, you need to find what works best for you. When you're training, your first step is to understand your 'why' by completing your self-assessment. Then you're ready to implement the right plan to achieve your goals. Property investing is the same. You need to act with the right property 'fit' for your strategy and long-term objectives. Everyone who wants to get fit can see the value of a personal trainer: they help you achieve your goals faster and prevent you from making mistakes that could hurt! It's the same with property: the right techniques, experience and industry knowledge can save you a lot of effort, a lot of heartache and a lot of pain.

You still need to do the hard work yourself, but with the right guidance on *how* to invest, *what* to invest in and *when* to buy, you'll put yourself in a much greater position for success, whether you're new to investing or a seasoned property investor.

Time and time again, I have seen investors searching for the 'perfect' property, the 'silver bullet' that will fast-track their success. I call these properties 'unicorns', because as cute as the idea sounds, they don't exist. So, how do you make the money you want out of property if these magical unicorn properties don't exist? There are so many ways to make money out of property, and so many gurus out there that it's hard to know who or what to listen to. Personally, I was so scared to trust anyone that I thought it would be safer to do it myself and learn as I went, despite it taking considerably longer than it would have if I'd had the *right* advisors. It did work for me, but sadly this isn't the case for everyone.

Many of the investors I work with have shared with me their goals, their fears, their financial situations and what *they* believe to be their pathway to riches. But I can see straight away that they're not thinking for the future, and this is what I love so much about what I do: I have a deep understanding of the lack of clarity most investors have about their long-term plans and know how to help them, how to structure everything and, of course, what property strategy to implement. Just as with any fitness instructor, the deeper my experience, the more I can help people on their own journey.

That's why I'm breaking it down to what's practical and achievable regardless of your risk profile and experience. In this book, I'll dive into eight of the most popular property investment strategies and discuss the positives and negatives for each, as well as exploring opportunities to build wealth with each. They're the strategies you've probably read about, and those your friends and family talk about. They're also those I've earmarked as being the most relevant to your life now. I don't know what's going to happen to the property markets in 2030 and beyond, but I can help you establish real and practical strategies today so you can begin investing like a professional.

How do I know these strategies work? I've spoken to and worked with literally thousands of people in my years of property investing. I've heard stories of what has worked and not worked, listened to people's fears and concerns, and understood how people make financial decisions. As I mentioned, I've also had amazing insight into how people's long-term wealth plans are ruined every single day. I feel privileged to have been able to take a snapshot of the general property market and know what the typical investor goes through, and why most fail. And let's not forget that I've learnt from my many mistakes, too!

Together, these insights inform Part I of the book. I share my experiences with you to illustrate that while there are no silver bullets, you can achieve great things with a rock-solid mindset. By getting real with yourself on exactly what you want to achieve from your investing and in your life, and combining that with proven systems and an expert team, you're much more likely to achieve exceptional results in your property investing career. And yes, it's a career. You're not going to become a millionaire overnight, nor are there any crazy, get-rich-quick schemes here. I make no apologies for that!

In Part II, I'll start with four of the easier strategies. These are what I call 'the easy fit'. You still need to do the work but, done correctly, they'll do the heavy lifting for you, so long as they fit with your plan. But I'm warning you – they're neither sexy nor unicorns! They're workhorses, but those you want in your stable. Often, less sexy is better. It's all about numbers, profit and growth, remember? Not high ceilings, pretty architraves, ocean views and swimming pools.

The next four strategies in Part III are higher-risk strategies – proceed with caution here. They're not for the fainthearted and carry more risk, but when done well they can be extremely lucrative. I'll share with you what you need to know and how to make them work, all with case studies and mentor tips on things I've learnt the hard way.

THE END IN MIND

Ultimately, my aim is to teach you how to become an elite investor. That means learning how to master the art of investing in property with the end in mind. This book is about determining the best pathway to success without taking on huge risks, or wasting time on activities or opportunities that may not produce a great result. As I always say, you can make money, but you can't get your time back. So, don't waste this precious resource on dud investments or the wrong strategy.

You might think it's easy for me to sit here and talk about all of this. Yes, I've been there, done that and lived to tell the tale. However, I'm here to tell you that the journey to get here certainly wasn't easy. There have been just as many challenges as there have been satisfying highs. The challenges were particularly difficult, and as I mentioned before, I made mistakes trying to work out how to become a successful property investor. The fact that I didn't have a coach or mentor to help me along the way in my own personal journey is a perfect example of the need for mentoring for long-term results.

But I'm a firm believer in learning something valuable every time you fail at something. In hindsight, these are the lessons that have made me into the investor that I am today. As I look back on my property investment journey, I hope that by sharing some of my mistakes, you can avoid making them too. For me, there's nothing worse than seeing a potentially fantastic investor undermined by poor education, inexperience, naivety and ignorance, all of which I suffered from when starting out.

By sharing these mistakes with you, I hope you can see that despite making some mistakes along the way, today I'm a successful investor with financial security and stability, and room for calculated risk with a confident outlook. I made it out the other side and didn't do it with a silver spoon in my mouth, or a silver bullet. I started out in life with a positive money mindset and a relentless attitude to achieve success when it came to building wealth. My insights have allowed me to refine my skills over the years, and I would argue that there are very few people in the country who do what we do here at The Property Mentors. It's an extremely fulfilling position to be in, and we have a lot of fun helping people every day.

Let me leave you with something I've never forgotten. When I was in grade six, my teacher (Mr Moy) used to repeat things so we would learn them. I clearly remember him saying, 'Repetition is boring, repetition is boring, repetition is boring.' He made the whole class repeat it over and over to highlight that it's the boring stuff that needs to sink in, because often that's what's important.

So, let me say this again: there's no silver bullet, there's no fast-track to riches and there are no unicorns! Don't be disappointed, though. You don't want those things anyway. After all, you don't know what you don't know.

Now, let's learn from my mistakes.

PART I

GETTING MATCH FIT

1

LEARNING FROM
MY MISTAKES – MY STORY

As a young kid growing up in suburban Perth, I was always thinking of creative ways to make money. I was full of ideas. The difference between me and my friends was that I did something about it, using my time on weekends and after school to try to bring my hair-brained schemes to life.

My first hustle was when I turned 12. It was a 'swap meet' in a car-park, based at my local Warwick Grove shopping centre, where I used to take bits and pieces of hard rubbish from people's curbsides and sell them for a profit. It took me hours to drag these things home during the week, and I couldn't believe people were throwing out perfectly good stuff when I could sell it and make a dollar or two.

From a young age, I learnt an invaluable life skill. I learnt how to negotiate with people – adults – because a lot of the people there were used to bartering competitively. I thought it was fun to get the win and a good deal. So, there I was, driving a hard bargain. I certainly didn't learn that in school! In fact, I hated school. Running the swap meets gave me an insight into how the real world worked from a young age, and it also taught me how to create a good business model.

Luckily, Mum and Dad were extremely supportive. Their garage was constantly full of my crap; Mum parked her car on one side of the garage, and I had my rubbish on the other. Dad had to park his car out in the driveway because my stuff took up all of the room. Looking back, I think I taught myself a lot about buying and selling, because my parents didn't really say to me, 'You should try this.' It was just me saying, 'Hey, I found a way to make some money, this is what I want to do.' And I'm so thankful that they supported me. It was lots of fun. In fact, looking back now, Mum and Dad were *incredibly* patient and supportive, even though it may not have been clear to them at the time what my plan was. I'm sure they said to each other, that's just Luke being Luke! (Actually, I know for a fact they still do.)

MY FIRST JOB

By the age of 16, I'd been working at Hungry Jack's for two years. I wanted more, so I decided to reach out and see a careers coordinator while at school to help me find me a job. At the time, I was really hating school and hungry to experience the real world (and start taking it over, or so I thought). I wanted to be an electrician (again, so I thought), so I sent out 80 or so letters trying to find a job. I've still got that list of places I sent letters to!

In the end, I left school at age 16 to do a traineeship with a company based in Carine, in the northern suburbs of Perth, one suburb over from where I was living in Marmion. Unfortunately, it was terrible! We had to sit in the back of the van with the toolboxes. There were two people in the front and one person in the back – it was completely unsafe. There were no seatbelts either, but this was just what happened back in 1997. On site, we used to stand on the top of two-storey roofs with no safety equipment, half a metre from the edge, pulling a tile off and dropping a cable down. I remember doing this on windy days, sunny days and days when it had been raining. I was standing on a two-storey roof, essentially risking my life for

$4.71 an hour. It was incredible, but it did teach me resilience – a lot of it! I left after about a year – the traineeship wasn't being run properly, and I considered it slave labour given that my Hungry Jack's job paid more.

This opened the door for me to seek work elsewhere, and I found it in West Perth, at a security company called Securus. I began to realise that I could work faster and more effectively than my colleagues. The job was for better money, and the company paid for my fuel, bought roof racks for my car and threw me in the deep end with complete autonomy. I was going out on my own to install security systems. But because I was always thinking one step ahead, I wanted to speed things up and investigate how I could make more money. I worked there for a while before becoming a contractor, taking the opportunity to increase my income.

PLANTING THE PROPERTY SEED

I approached Brett Clugston – who was my mate's dad in high school and my boss at Securus – and said, 'How can I make some more money? I thought I'd be earning more money by now.' He responded with two things I've never forgotten. The first was, 'Luke, disappointment is the difference between expectation and reality.' So, I'm not getting a pay rise, I thought. The other was, 'Luke, go and buy a block of land somewhere and just pay it off. In the future, that'll be a good thing for you, so just get started.'

It was the first time anybody had given me property advice, full stop – even though it was quite generic and not tailored to my goals. But I'd never really considered it before. I sat back and gave it some thought. On a $14,500 salary, buying anything over $5000 wasn't really an option for me at that point – except for my car, which I loved.

However, it was great advice, and while I didn't really take it on board at the time, it planted the seed and gave me something to think about seriously later, when I was ready. I had always loved property, but without knowing how to even get started, nothing happened. The gaps between where I was at in life, my financial situation and the reality of buying a block of land were just far too big.

A1 SECURE SOLUTIONS

In three years, I had left school and started as a trainee, worked on the tools for another company, gone into the office for a pay rise, added weekend work and then doubled my income by becoming a contractor. The lightbulb moment arrived when I suddenly thought, 'Why am I doing all this work for *their* clients when I could go and get my *own* clients and build my *own* business?'

At 19, I decided to do just that. I got myself a logo, phone number, horrible website, fax number and business cards. I even had a pager – how ridiculous! Well, at the time they were cool. But more importantly, I was in business. I named it A1 Secure Solutions, and I was on my way. Over the next few years, I focused on growth and learnt how to build a business. At one point I had three vans on the road and owned a 2001 Monaro, which was my pride and joy. I was killing it and life was good. That was a huge amount of risk for someone my age to take on, but I loved the challenge and it was light years ahead of the alternative, which was working for someone else.

MY FIRST PROPERTY

It was 1999 and I was about to turn 20, and ready to make my debut on the Australian property market. I found the right place, too: a four-bedroom, one-bathroom property on a 682 m² block in the Perth suburb of Duncraig. The house was small but solid, and as it was my first, I didn't care about pools or double storeys. I just wanted to get started. It cost me $157,500.

To save for the deposit, I worked harder than I ever had before. I employed staff, secured extra tools, ran advertisements in the local paper, did letterbox drops and whatever else I could to get my business any work that was out there. I finally managed to scrape together about $20,000, and I had my deposit. But as I soon discovered, there were pitfalls to being self-employed, because the banks didn't like my employment status.

Luckily, Mum and Dad stepped in and went guarantor on my loan, which caused me to miss out on the newly announced first home buyers grant: $7000. This would have gone a long way back then! Again, I didn't care, I just wanted to get started. And the upshot was that I was now the owner of my first property! I was always surprised that being self-employed made it difficult to get a loan, but my staff could qualify for a loan after three months of employment.

My plan was to spend the next six to 12 months renovating it. I had tradie mates to help me, and I used my swap-meet skills to buy things that people were selling cheaply or giving away online or in local newspapers. For example, people would give away palm trees or rocks, so I acquired them and put them in the garden. I also learnt from a young age that all the expensive houses in Perth had lights in their gardens, but the average suburban houses didn't have any. I figured that something I could do was install lights in the garden, because at night-time they would stand out and highlight the plants, making the property look more expensive. Lighting also makes a property feel welcoming, creating good street appeal. Plus, I love gardening, and how nice it is to come home after a long day at work and see the garden all lit up.

Looking back, I think I was the only one in the street to have garden lighting, which were little LED things that would fade out after two hours. They quickly got replaced by proper 240-volt lights. It looked great. Not to blow my own trumpet here, but it soon became the best house in the street, and I was proud to come home every day.

I also used a good cashflow strategy for this property. Of the four bedrooms, I used one as the office and one as my room, but

I rented out the other two bedrooms to help pay the mortgage. That netted me around $80 per week per room, which helped fund the renovations.

The mistake

The advice I was given at this time was, 'Buy and hold, and pay off your debt.' Sure, this made a lot of sense to me, and that's why I spent weekends and nights pulling up gardens, painting, scaping floors and doing what felt like a never-ending renovation while I was living in the Duncraig property, trying to make it 'home'. At the same time, I started paying down the debt like I was told. But following that advice initially was a mistake, because after I'd finished the renovation, I realised I could add value and pull equity out. This was easier back in the early 2000s, with banks being more lenient with this type of strategy. Friends and family were constantly popping over to check out the latest work, and many of them got their hands dirty, for which I will be forever grateful.

MY SECOND PROPERTY

A couple of years later, in 2003, I decided to sell A1 Secure Solutions, rent out the Duncraig property and move to Sydney to take a full-time job on a good salary. Now 23, I wanted to invest in more property. But I was hitting brick walls with the banks because it was tough securing finance as a business owner. I was beginning to get a taste of how the banks' policies could affect my lending ability. I had equity, but it wasn't enough. For me, Sydney offered job stability and borrowing capacity, which the banks love, plus the opportunity to progress my investing career.

Three months after I'd finished my probation with my new Sydney job in security, I had a finance application to buy property number two back in Western Australia. I was 24. Like a lot of investors, I bought in an area that I knew, and as easy as that, I was officially a 'property investor' with a 'property portfolio'. How fancy!

The mistake

Buying my second property, I made one of the most common mistakes I see today: I bought in an area that I knew. This is a short-sighted strategy because it doesn't necessarily represent excellent value or growth as an investment. It simply provides a false sense of security because you're more familiar with the area than the next person, but it won't necessarily yield better results than investing in another area. Instead, you need to take emotion out of buying property – full stop. Successful property investment is a game of numbers and statistics rather than heart and soul. It's harder, because it may feel strange to buy something in a place you've never visited, but when you're looking at profit, it's the mindset you need to adopt to become successful. The challenge for most investors is that they wouldn't know where to start looking outside of areas they already know. And I was no different.

MY THIRD PROPERTY

Enter the Tasmania house.

After 13 months in Sydney, I was offered the opportunity to relocate to Melbourne to open my employer's new state office. I took it. I was living in South Yarra and working in Doncaster. With my two-property portfolio, I had confidence, and it was time to try something out of left field. So, I went and bought a house in a mining town: Queenstown, Tasmania. I was reading Steve McKnight's book *From 0 to 130 Properties in 3.5 Years* and, like a lot of people, thought that's how you must invest because this guy has written it in a book. In hindsight, I blindly followed the strategy without knowing if it was the right fit for me.

I bought the property for the bargain price of $79,500, and I rented it out at $120 per week. But then the property started to pack up, with problem after problem forcing me to continually fork out money to fix it. The property became a charity case, and by the time

I sold it I'd made nothing and there was no capital growth. Thankfully, with all the swings and roundabouts, I didn't lose any money in the end and was able to claim some depreciation benefits. But it was more hassle than it was worth. I really did learn a lot from that one! Basically, the property was an extremely steep learning curve, with more dips than upward trajectories. I share more about this experience in Chapter 5.

The mistake

If a property book presents you with a silver bullet, it doesn't mean you *should* follow the strategy. Just because you *can* do something, it doesn't mean you should do it. Granted, you're reading a property book right now, but the strategies that I recommend are based around you as the investor and finding the right *property fit*, rather than the property itself. A property may be cheap, providing a cash-positive scenario, but you may have to spend more money – like I did – in the long run, and ultimately it may not help you to achieve your goals.

THE FOURTH PROPERTY

In 2005, I bought a house in Bonbeach, Melbourne. It wasn't beachfront, and it had an old granny flat out the back that was so run-down the agent wouldn't even walk through it. There were rats running around, and it was probably full of asbestos, too. The agent couldn't sell the property – until they met me. I can be pretty optimistic when taking on a project! But when I offered my price – $260,000 – and the valuer headed there to do a valuation, the bank concluded that it wouldn't lend on the property because there was no kitchen or bathroom. The former owners were part way through renovating the bathroom, so everything had been ripped out and the place was falling to bits. I said to the vendor that I wanted to knock $5000 off the price because I was going to have to install a kitchen and bathroom, and that I also needed access to the property before settlement. They agreed to that, and then I jumped onto eBay and spent less than $1000 on kitchen and bathroom items. I got $5000 off the price, only spent $1000 and had a working kitchen and bathroom before settlement. They were terrible, but they got me over the line in the end. The valuer came out again and valued it at the contract price, with the bank ultimately saying, 'You've got the property.' I was over the moon.

The mistake

I submitted a planning permit through the local council to subdivide the block into two townhouses. That part was straightforward, but it took a very long time as the council wanted countless changes, and the costs just kept racking up as we went back and forth. The tricky part was the granny flat out the back, which I had to demolish, but I made it work. In the end, I sold the Bonbeach property in 2010 and replaced it with a beautiful direct-beachfront home in Carrum, not far away. I love that house, and it's still part of my property portfolio and earning a great rental return.

This deal taught me how to negotiate, and that there are different ways to put property deals together. Too often, people make the mistake of just accepting what the bank tells them and thinking that the deal is off, but in this case, I learnt what the bank was looking for and what would ultimately get my deal over the line. Of course, this experience also gave me more confidence when dealing with the banks, and that could only be a good thing! The other lesson to take from this project was that delays usually cost you money and time, which can quickly erode your profits.

THE FIFTH, SIXTH, SEVENTH PROPERTIES AND BEYOND...

In 2007, I bought a property in Seaford which was a development site. I wanted something I could knock down and build two units on. Like a lot of investors, I wanted to fast-track my portfolio. Thinking this was the best way, I went out there to find a property in an affordable location where there was a precedent for this type of small development.

Not long after I bought the property in Seaford, I went to Las Vegas on a business trip for my security business, Monitored Alarms, which I had been running since 2005. One very late night, after many drinks on the Strip, I saw a television show where people renovated houses and then built in the house's backyard. It was a lightbulb moment. 'Luke – what have you done!?' I said to myself. 'Why did you buy a house that needs knocking down? Why didn't you buy one where you could *keep* the front house and just renovate it? Oh no!'

I returned to Melbourne, called my real estate agent and told him to list the property for sale, just months after I had bought it. Luckily, I was able to find a buyer to take the property off my hands relatively quickly, and I even made a small profit – enough to cover my initial stamp duty and selling costs.

After that, I found a property in a superior location (closer to the train station) in the same suburb, on a bigger block and in a nice quiet street. There was also the opportunity to build in the back-yard. I bought it and started working on plans and permits to build the brand-new unit in the backyard, which I completed in 2010.

The mistake

The lesson here is that trying to fast-track can cost time and money, and work against you by slowing you down. I also learnt that having a top agent on your side is good, but they'll only ever follow your instructions. I asked for a property that I could knock down and build two units on, and that's what I got. Now that I look back at it, the numbers on that development were never going to stack up, so it wouldn't have made any money at all. Of course, I didn't know that at the time; I just thought I wanted to be a developer! It wasn't until after a night out in Las Vegas, a bunch of drinks and some very late-night television that I realised I had my strategy wrong. Imagine if I could have avoided these mistakes altogether! But you live and learn.

MY MONUMENTAL LIFE SHIFT

With a bunch of properties now under my belt, I continued to buy more every year. By this stage, I was helping friends with their renovations, doing multiple renovations of my own, and continuing to run Monitored Alarms and make good money. Like a lot of investors, I was trying my very best to manufacture growth and accelerate my wealth creation. I didn't know any better, but I was jumping from one thing to the next and hoping it would all work out. And so far it was, but it was a bit of a mismatched and unplanned portfolio because there was no end point with any of the properties.

And then I had my (sort of) mid-/quarter-life crisis. As I outlined in the preface, it was a huge wake-up call. It turns out I didn't want fancy cars or first-class travel, I just wanted what most people seek – financial stability and financial freedom. It was such a revelation to me because it took me deeper into myself to a place that was authentic and genuine. I came to really understand what *I* valued – I, alone – which was the important factor. I spent a long 18 months re-evaluating my life, and by the end of it I was 100 per cent clear on what I wanted out of life from that point on: financial stability and financial freedom. It was such a bittersweet moment: I knew what I wanted; I just wish I'd figured it out sooner.

But how did I do it?

Despite my mistakes, I realised that success through buying property was absolutely possible. It wasn't pie-in-the-sky stuff – it was achievable, and I could do it myself, but it relied on excellent planning and time. I wanted a house, so I spoke to some mortgage brokers and the bank, saved a deposit, got finance, and bought it. To me, nothing else mattered apart from saving the deposit, and

I did whatever it took. Nowadays, I speak to young people who like the idea of getting into property. I tell them they need to sacrifice two years or more to save up for a deposit, but they don't want to do it. They walk around with their $2000 iPhone in their pockets, and I wonder where their priorities lie. They don't want to make any sacrifices and, sadly, they want it all now. (Listen to me as the old and wise 41-year-old!)

I learnt from a young age that if I wanted to make money, I had to make sacrifices – delayed gratification. I had to get out of my comfort zone. Don't get me wrong, there were times I wasn't home until 3am and I had to get up at 5am on a Saturday morning with a hangover ready for work, but that's how I learnt. If you make the sacrifices, set out a plan and have that deep desire to achieve your goals, you can make it work.

Now, let's talk about you and how you can take your first steps to find the right property fit.

2

RECAP OF *LET'S GET REAL* – WHY MOST INVESTORS FAIL

After writing *Let's Get Real*, the need for this book became clear.

All day, people tell me, 'Luke – I have my goals documented, I now know my "dreams, dates and dollars" (as I outlined in that book), but what properties should I be looking at? How do I know what to do next?'

What I'm actually hearing is that investors want to try to fast-track the process. They want to get from A to Z without doing B, C, D, E and all the other steps. People come in and say, 'Oh, I've got $100,000 equity and I want to be a developer,' or, 'I've done this course to do flips and wraps and whatever other strategies are out there,' or, 'I'm 58 years old and I've done a course on renovations, and that's what I want to do. I don't even own a hammer, but that's what I want to do.'

Hold up.

There are a lot of people who think they've got a silver bullet for property success. It reminds me of when I was starting out and I felt that people needed someone to put all these ideas into context. They're reading pages and pages of literature about it, and watching investors on television talk up the market, and then trying to find out what suits them, all the while getting sucked in by spruikers. Of course, there are all sorts of weird and wonderful tactics out there for people to try their hand at, but which ones actually work? And what do most investors actually need?

The thing is, most people investing in property in Australia start out the same way. They collect some money in cash, equity or a self-managed superannuation fund and head out looking for a 'deal' – the 'perfect' property that will help them to build wealth and achieve all their goals.

This short-sighted vision is often why many investors fail to get the results they desire. When challenged by things out of their control, they simply forget about the end goal and never reach Point B. Often, that's because their Point B was never clearly articulated in the first place.

This pivotal concept provided the premise for my first book, *Let's Get Real*. In this book, the focus was on you as the investor, clarifying your goals and working out your 'why', just as I did. As mentors, we also work on your plans and your mindset, which can each influence your success as a property investor. Most investors fail because they fail to plan. The book recognised that we all have different dreams, desires and goals in life, and that to achieve those exceptional results you need to apply different pathways rather than a single right way. Not everyone needs a $10 million property portfolio, so why aim for that? Remember, it's the *result* you're ultimately after, not the property itself. When you let your emotions get in the way, that's where you come unstuck.

After 20 years of buying property, my message – as I said earlier – is that there are no silver bullets. I mean, some silver bullet strategies do work for some people, some of the time, but it's more about doing it the right way, with the right processes in place, and creating a pathway to profit that is slower and steadier, rather than reactive and rushed.

I can tell you that the magical unicorn property simply does not exist, either. And this fundamental fact is what separates professional property investors with long-term sustainable wealth from those who are simply out dabbling in property investments and hoping that it all works out. Remember, we are here to talk about investing, not speculating. We are here to talk about long-term wealth creation, not making a quick buck, or trying to buy low and sell high and pick the market.

Let's go back a step. The key message from my first book was to work out your 'why' and why your 'why' matters. Essentially, your 'why' is everything. I encouraged you to think about the book as a 'why-to' guide, so that your investment success is more about good planning and tactical execution rather than a lack of access to technical information.

I also wrote the book to give you a chance to learn about your emotional self and to master all of those emotions that may hold you back from achieving your goals. Because if you're going to become a property investor, you'll need to strap yourself in and ask yourself some tough questions first.

PROPERTY INVESTMENT PROFILE

Before you skip to Part II and consider the best property fit for you, you will need to work out your property investment profile. Think of it as a self-assessment exercise that you must fill out to see which strategies will suit you best. I highly advise you to think carefully about where you sit, because these responses will help to guide your best fit in property investing.

What is your risk profile?

How risky is the investment based on your age, financial position, and knowledge and understanding of the strategy? What suits one investor can be a complete disaster for another. Your risk profile will likely change as you increase your education and experience.

What is your asset position?

Depending on the strategy, you will likely need some sort of security to offer a lender. This doesn't always have to be another property, but this is typically the most attractive to lenders. Often, the more risk involved in the strategy, the more security the lender requires.

What is your cash position?

You will need some skin in the game. Depending on the strategy, you'll either need a small amount of capital to get started or you might need access to *lots* of capital. Regardless, I always recommend having good buffers in place for a rainy day, because I promise you that it does rain, and you will need access to cash.

What is your exit strategy?

Successful investing takes time, energy and patience, but you need to have an idea of your exit strategy before parting with money in any investment. Of course, for most people, this is one of the hardest things to calculate because there are many unknowns; however, this is a crucial component to successful investing.

How much time do you have?

Property investing can be an almost entirely passive investment, partly hands-on, or an all-hands-on-deck game! How much time you have available will be an important factor to determine which strategies are best for your personal situation. As for time, this is not something you should try to 'squeeze into' your current lifestyle. Investing in property is something that needs clear and focused time if you're looking for the best results. You either have the time to do it properly, or you don't.

THE THREE STAGES OF READINESS

How do you know you're ready to invest? There are three fundamental components to being truly 'ready' to invest, which I call 'the three stages of readiness'. These three stages are vital to acknowledge before going out into the marketplace. While you don't always need to be 100 per cent ready in each of these areas, being aware of their existence and how they can affect your results is extremely important.

1. *Financially ready:* Every investor needs some capital to work with, so you need to be financially ready to get into the property market and start investing. Not all property strategies require a lot of capital, however it certainly helps and gives you more options. Not only do you need to have some funds available to invest, but you will also need to ensure your financial house is in order, plus have a good credit score, little or no bad debt, and a financial buffer.

2. *Emotionally ready:* Yes, emotions are important when it comes to successful property investing. But I'm not talking about your emotions taking control; it's more that you need to be emotionally connected to your investment goals, because there will be times when you've had enough and will want to give up. Being emotionally ready means you're in control of your emotions and connected enough with the end goal to get out of your comfort zone.

3. *Educationally ready:* Education is key, but of course education must be specific to the goals you wish to achieve. This doesn't mean you have to be an expert on everything property before you're ready; however, it does help that you have the education behind you that aligns with your goals. Essentially, you need specific education rather than broad-based education that may not be relevant to you.

It amazes me how many people are blasé about building wealth in property and want to do it all on their own. Personally, this was what I did in my early 20s when I was just getting started, because I didn't think I 'needed' help. Buying a property simply involved signing a contract and getting a loan, right? Over my property investing career, I've learnt that the actual act of buying property is easy, but investing successfully and achieving sustainable long-term results is the hard part.

If you haven't already, it will help to read my previous book *Let's Get Real* first, to get a clear understanding of your goals and, specifically, why you're doing this in the first place. Assuming you have completed your property investment profile and are aware of where you sit in 'the three stages of readiness' (well done), let's get started determining the strategy that is right for you. It's time to move forward!

LINE UP YOUR DUCKS

Most people wrongly assume the first step is to go out in the marketplace, start looking at property, snap up a great deal and jump onto the ladder. And while the strategies in this book will also largely depend on your goals and time frames, you need to make sure you have the appropriate financial capacity to invest first. That's why the first step for most investing strategies is finance. You need money – preferably lots of it, but small amounts can turn into big amounts if done right. I understand that not everyone has boxes of spare cash locked away under the bed!

So, you need to get all your ducks lined up and ensure your finance strategy is in place first. Having your finances sorted means that you'll not only be armed with the right information about your lending options to secure your property, but you'll also be in a much stronger position to negotiate. Plus, it could prevent you from paying too much or entering into a contract you can't get funding for. You might also be able to secure more funding than you first thought, which could allow you to consider more properties or provide better flexibility with your offers. See how much sense that makes?

When speaking with your mortgage broker, make sure you ask lots of questions about your upcoming purchase. Be upfront and honest, too, because open and transparent communication is the only way to work with your expert team. Don't think that not disclosing that credit card or the stash of money under your bed is a good idea – this information is vital and could make a huge difference to your credit application. After all, your broker is on your side – their reason for being part of your expert team is to help you succeed and assist you with building wealth. Don't forget that a good broker will be there to help you long-term, so you need to think smart and futureproof that relationship – it works both ways.

Mentor tip

The questions you need to ask your broker at this point revolve more around you than the property itself. For example, how will your borrowing capacity be affected if you pay off your car loan or credit card, or if you earn extra overtime or obtain a second job? These things can make a big difference to the result and, of course, can vary massively between lenders.

SET UP YOUR STRUCTURE

Once you have your finances in order, your next job is to manage risk by setting up the right structures or entities. These are the financial frameworks you'll use to buy your property, which will also provide a certain layer of asset protection – and peace of mind in case things go wrong. Before you buy the property, you will need to know what name you're buying in. This is often known as the 'purchasing entity', so make sure you have discussed this with your accountant as this will affect your lending options. Where possible, get your accountant and broker on the phone together to discuss the best outcome for you. This needs to happen *before* you sign any contracts and *before* you apply for any loans. Lenders treat your finance application very differently depending on what the purchasing entity is, so it's not something you can decide at the last minute, or your broker may not be very happy with you. Not all investors and not all strategies require bulletproof structures in place, but in some cases they are absolutely necessary and you would be ill-advised to buy property assets in your own name. For others, it's entirely appropriate to buy in your own name and the tax advantages make it worthwhile.

For all eight strategies discussed in this book, there are varying levels of risk. Obviously there's financial risk, but some strategies involve risk to you personally. As if the risk of losing money wasn't bad enough, imagine getting sued for something that isn't your fault! It happens more often than you might think, so getting the right structures in place first is very important. Again, these are important steps to take to become a professional long-term investor.

Some of the most common structures and entities that you could use include:

- family trusts
- unit trusts
- hybrid trusts
- companies
- self-managed superannuation funds (SMSFs)
- personal name/s.

While these entities are the most common, they don't suit everyone. Over the years, I've met dozens of investors who have complex, sophisticated and probably bulletproof asset protection structures, but they've spent so much money setting them up that they've got nothing left to invest. I wish I was joking, but I see it all the time. It's sad to see people being taken advantage of like that.

Furthermore, lending varies for each of the above, and there can be some huge differences in lending options, deposits required and, of course, your personal risk. For example, lending in an SMSF is non-recourse lending, which does not carry any personal risk to you as the assets held in the SMSF are separate to your other assets. However, SMSF lending typically requires a deposit of between

20 and 40 per cent (or more), and interest rates are a little higher because there are currently fewer lenders that have an appetite for this type of finance. This may change in the future, of course. And this isn't a bad thing; it's a cost of doing business as far as I'm concerned. For the sake of an extra 0.5 to 1 per cent to secure a good asset, it certainly doesn't stop me investing.

When you're starting out, accountants will often recommend buying properties in your own name for tax purposes. This isn't necessarily a bad idea, as it gets you started and onto the playing field, but of course your long-term plans for the property are also important, so you need to be clear with your accountant from the outset and outline exactly what your intentions are before signing any contracts.

My rule is that it's *always* best to discuss your upcoming purchase with your broker, and then loop your accountant into the conversation to get your purchase in the right name/s. This seems like a lot of 'boring' work and it's not as much fun as checking out properties to buy, but remember that you're investing like a professional, and a little upfront work before you proceed can save you thousands of dollars in the future.

Mentor tip

Setting up the appropriate structures before you buy your investment can save you a small fortune in the future!

Case study

Lynne is in her 60s and purchased a property in the inner-eastern suburbs of Melbourne back in the 1980s. She lived in the property but eventually moved out (not selling it) and bought another one in a neighbouring suburb, where she has been ever since. Both properties have increased significantly in value, partly due to their great locations but also because

Melbourne's population has soared in the last 30 to 40 years. While demand for inner-city housing has gone gangbusters, there are a couple of issues that are now affecting Lynne's investments.

Lynne has always done the right thing by her tenants and maintained the property herself, rather than using a licensed property manager. One implication of this is that Lynne lets the tenants pay her directly, which has saved her some money along the way, but it means that unfortunately she's behind the market rate for the property by around $200 per week – that's over $10,000 a year she's been missing out on. The tenants have lived there for 18 years and they have a good relationship with Lynne, always paying on time. Lynne is happy to have these tenants in the property because they are no hassle, and they also look after the place. She's now paid off the mortgage, so the rental income is supporting her, and she doesn't want to mess with that.

The problem is that the property has significantly increased in value. How can that be a problem, you ask? Well firstly, because Lynne has paid off the property, she no longer has any interest deductions. Secondly, she's made virtually no improvements (renovations or major works) to the property, so there are no depreciation benefits; and, of course, she's around 30 per cent behind market rents for the area. Also, because she owns two more valuable investment properties in the same state, her land tax bill *alone* is more than $30,000 every year. Every. Single. Year.

This could have been avoided had Lynne obtained good advice before she secured these assets. Let me explain using a simplified example. Land tax is calculated so that every property you own in the same name (or entity) in the same state is added one on top of another. So, if you have three properties worth $500,000 each, the state revenue office will add them together so you are taxed on the *land value* of the properties combined (as shown in figure 2.1). In this example, you would be taxed on the *land value* of the $1.5 million portfolio. As land is taxed at greater rates the higher its value, this would mean a much higher tax bill. The scary part is that if you're a long-term investor, the properties are likely to increase in value, and as such, your land tax bill will continue to rise as you get older. The correct planning upfront can save you a small fortune in the future.

Figure 2.1: Land tax

Three separate entities each worth $500,000 (land value $250,000)

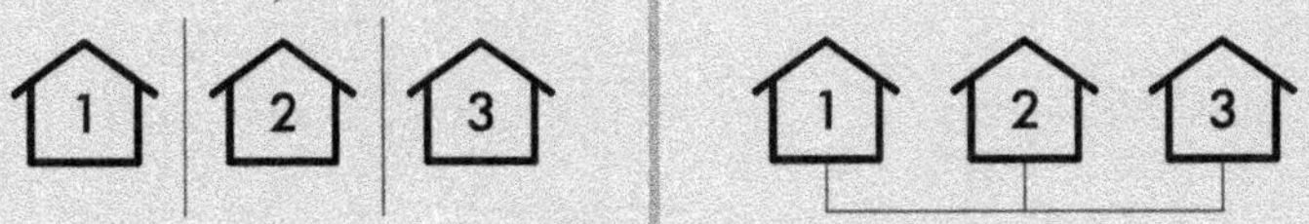

Taxation rate: $275
+ 0.2% of amount >$250,000
= $500 x 3 = $1500

Three properties all owned by the same entity totalling $1,500,000

Taxation rate: $2975
+ 0.8% of amount >$1,000,000
= $10,975

NB: The land tax figures used in this example are correct for Victoria at the time of writing, but keep in mind that all states and territories have some form of land tax!

With the right planning, you can take greater control of your destiny and succeed in the property game, whether you're a first-timer or already a seasoned investor. Next, it's time to assemble your expert team.

3

ASSEMBLING YOUR EXPERT TEAM

Any sporting coach worth their salt will tell you that you can't win with a team that can't work together for a common goal. In property parlance, the same philosophy applies. So, when we talk about assembling your expert team, we're talking about your 'core wealth team'. These aren't the external consultants you call in as a one-off, but rather the longer-term team of professionals you want by your side, helping you navigate your way through the property waters with the ability to act on your behalf when it comes to tricky decisions.

Ultimately, having the right team of experts around you, regardless of the investment strategy you ultimately choose, is fundamental to your success. Let me repeat that for those who were half asleep while reading that!

Having the right team of experts around you, regardless of the investment strategy you ultimately choose, is fundamental.

Your expert team is a group of professional people who each specialise in their field. They have been there and done that with clients doing what you want to achieve. It's worth remembering that not all mortgage brokers deal with investors daily, not all accountants specialise in property accounting and asset protection, and not all financial planners will even talk to you about property.

This can be tricky, and novice investors trip themselves up every day by going out there and talking to 'experts' to build wealth for them. They get advice from friends and family and trust that the person is 'good'. But are they? Do they know their stuff?

> Person 1: *'My best friend's sister's boyfriend's roommate is an accountant. He is a great guy; you should give him a call.'*
>
> Person 2: *'That's great! I'm not looking for the best advice, I just want someone who is a great person! Is he a property investor himself?'*
>
> Person 1: *'I don't think so, but he got me nearly $1500 back on my tax last year – he's amazing!'*
>
> Person 2: *'OMG $1500 – wow!'*

OK, so you get my point. I'm being a bit silly here with this exaggeration, but I hear this story time and time again, and unfortunately it costs people the two most precious things when it comes to long-term wealth creation:

1. It costs time.
2. It costs money.

Here are the real people you want in your corner.

MORTGAGE BROKER

Different strategies require very different approaches to your lending situation. We will cover this later, but let me drill this point home now: you need an excellent mortgage broker on your team, full stop! It means you need to be super careful when choosing your mortgage broker, because your broker is the person who could quite literally make or break your financial situation. The process of buying a property to live in as an owner-occupier is very different to that of most of the strategies we will cover in this book, so you need to work with an expert to ensure you take the right approach for your property investment strategy.

Now, while most mortgage brokers have good intentions (I would hope), not all are specialist investment professionals, and many don't even own property. You'd think it'd be helpful to have some personal experience when it comes to the work you choose to do, especially when you're helping clients build a successful portfolio and apply for commercial finance or development funding. But the reality is that my team and I have worked with dozens of mortgage brokers over the years and, to be blunt, some are useless. The good ones are very hard to find because they generally don't need to advertise. I've had to invest too much time educating brokers on how I want deals structured and presented to the lender because they didn't under-stand the complexities of my portfolio. Frustrating.

Another issue is that a lot of investors will opt to work with a mort-gage broker who has been referred by their friends, family or the local real estate agent. Often, this is a recipe for disaster.

Mentor tip

Just because a mortgage broker has a business card and a laptop does not mean they are suitably qualified to give you the best financial advice. So, ask lots of questions to ensure they know what they are doing.

Here are a few suggestions for how you can tell if your potential mortgage broker is the real deal:

- The obvious thing that all property investors should ask a mortgage broker is about their background in lending. Ask them straight out: 'How long have you been a mortgage broker?' This is often information you can discover from a bit of innocent online 'stalking' on LinkedIn or even on their own website, but it's extremely important to know this before you get too far into the conversation with them. If you can't find this information from your stalking efforts, simply ask them!

- Once you've established they aren't fresh out of mortgage-broker school, ask what *specific* experience they have with investor lending. Add to this by asking what split of their business (loans written) are for property investors. Personally, I would only work with a mortgage broker that deals with property investors 90 to 100 per cent of the time. Investor lending and portfolio planning is a very niche space, and few mortgage brokers have the skills and knowledge necessary to get you the very best results. If your broker largely deals with 'mum-and-dad' or 'vanilla' lending, then they probably aren't the best fit for you to build a successful portfolio.

- Here's another question you can ask which may seem obvious: 'Are you a property investor yourself?' If they answer 'no', it doesn't necessarily mean they won't be able to assist you; however, if your broker has been there and done that with their own money, they are more likely to understand what you're going through. This gives them more of the hands-on, 'real world' experience that's hard to put an exact value on but can add massive value to your portfolio growth. It's worth remembering it's the small tweaks we make as professional investors that ultimately net the best results.

Don't be scared to ask these questions! You're a serious investor looking to get serious results, so make sure you're comfortable with the answers you receive before proceeding. Don't be shy!

TAX ACCOUNTANT AND FINANCIAL PLANNER

Similarly, your accountant and financial planner play a critical role in your success. These professionals will help you ensure you have the correct tax minimisation strategies in place – better to have money in your pocket than in the tax department's. Your accountant can also consider options for asset protection, and how to get the best results from your superannuation fund through additional contributions and using the tax laws to your advantage.

As you build your portfolio and potentially move into more advanced property strategies over time, tax planning and structuring becomes more complicated, so tax accountants and financial planners are critical to your success. After all, as a professional property investor, you're building wealth for life, not just trying to make a quick buck – right?

While I have a strong bias for investing in property (obviously), for some people it may be appropriate to diversify into other asset classes, such as stocks or shares, bonds or precious metals as part of their wealth-creation plan. As a rule of thumb, successful investors around the world invest in what they understand. If you don't understand the investment, don't do it – or at least ask a million questions before you make a decision.

Receiving a good tax return is entirely different from receiving good tax minimisation advice, putting solid structures in place, and asset protection. Good advisors will talk to each other and have your best interests at heart, so ensure you secure the very best people on your side. A lot of people wrongly assume that their accountant is there to help them build wealth. I don't know where this urban legend came from, but it's a dangerous assumption. Your accountant is there to help you manage your tax affairs, and this may include setting up various entities and structures for you, but their role is to do just that, not to give you investment advice.

Your financial planner can also assist you with SMSFs, investing in the stock market, life (and death) insurance, total and permanent disability (TPD) insurance and other insurances to plan for the future.

The only issue I have with the financial planning industry is that financial planners are not able to recommend direct property for investment. The residential housing market in Australia is worth some $7 trillion or more, yet financial planners cannot recommend this asset class. Strange, hey? They are literally giving you advice on how to set up and plan for your financial future, so why can't they talk about property?

The reason for this is that financial planners sell products, which are packaged up with disclaimers and product disclosure statements (PDSs). It would be ridiculously labour-intensive and inefficient for financial planners to prepare a PDS for each of the 10 million or more residential properties out there – so they simply don't. Furthermore, financial planners can often make ongoing commissions for money you have invested with them. If they recommended residential property, they may make a one-off commission, but they · can't make any money off you again.

Personally, I think investors need to understand the role of having a financial planner in their team. As much as I respect the good ones out there, there are many who are simply glorified salespeople selling insurance and investment products – as with any industry, there are some great financial planners and there are some terrible ones. But financial planners are important for everyone building wealth, and at some point you're going to need one on your team. There are some excellent financial planners out there who are happy to work with you on your property portfolio and are quite often property investors themselves.

Lastly, just as with a tattoo artist, don't try to screw your accountant or financial planner on fees. Good advice is worth paying for, because the results, like a tattoo, can last a lifetime.

Mentor tip

Choosing the right accountant and financial planner is key to your success. As with your mortgage broker, you want to ask questions about their level of experience assisting property investors. Ask what experience they have in portfolio planning and structuring, and how they believe they can 'add value' to your situation beyond the day-to-day accounting or insurance requirements.

BUILDER

If there's an industry where everyone has an opinion, and it's usually a bad one, it's the building industry. Most of us have had a questionable experience with builders (or know someone who has): they didn't show up when they said they would, they didn't quote properly and then stung you for a big bill at job completion or they just flat-out did crappy work.

It's so important to do your due diligence when choosing a builder. There are some amazing properties out there, and some very, very bad ones. In figure 3.1, on page 41, someone came up with the designs, the builder quoted on them, the client signed off and the jobs went ahead. The problems are obvious, of course. The door is half a metre off the ground, and the windows... well, what can you say! From start to finish, nobody considered the results and spoke up. But it's the clients who have invested a huge amount of money and time into the projects that they'll never get back.

Mentor tip

When engaging a builder, one of the most important things you can do is inspect their previous work.

Of course, any builder will be happy to show you a recent project they have built. You can either do this in person, where the builder may do a drive-by with you in the car, or you can also jump onto their website and have a look at their portfolio or gallery. See if they've won any awards, too – specifically from industry associations such as the Housing Industry Association (HIA) or Master Builders Australia (MBA). To really take this to the next level, ask to see a project they built five or even ten years ago. See how it's standing the test of time, and whether it looks structurally and cosmetically sound. Don't be afraid to knock on the door and speak to whoever is living there, either. Ask if there are any problems with the quality of the home – most people will be happy to tell you if there are any problems. If there are, go back to the builder and see how they respond – their answer should help guide your decision!

A WINNING FORMULA

Only the top 5 per cent of investors can produce stellar results. That's not many! And even fewer can build long-term sustainable wealth that provides *income for life*. But they aren't 'lucky', and they aren't people who 'bought well'. They're simply people like you who had a plan and a strategy to match their goals, with an expert core wealth team to assist them on their journey. They also have the staying power to hold on for the long-term. As I said at the start of this chapter, property investing is a team sport, a journey, and there is no fast way to riches. Those who try to take shortcuts usually find themselves at a dead end, and must turn around and start again.

Assembling an expert team to work harmoniously with you towards your end goal is a far better outcome, and you'll need to speak to a *lot* of experts – and, of course, ask the right questions – to find the right people. Believe me, I have worked with dozens of experts over the years. Some are as useless as a bikini on a bull, and for only a fraction more you can get someone with advice that's light years ahead. The difference at the end can be incredible.

Just as all builders aren't the same, not all advisors are the same. Compare the buildings in figure 3.1 to the buildings in figure 3.2.

All clients ended up with a house at the end, but I'm sure you will agree that the outcomes look very different. If you use the wrong experts, and if you don't get involved in the process and ask questions along the way, your property portfolio may end up with a door you can't use or windows that are misaligned – or somewhere between the two examples. At The Property Mentors, we prefer that our members learn and become educated through the process. If you're asking better questions, you will start getting better answers over time, and in the long run you're more likely to get better results!

Figure 3.1: Two examples of very bad building projects

*Figure 3.2: An example of a well coordinated,
professionally built project*

THE LAST WORD

Your expert team comprises multiple people: a mortgage broker, an accountant, a financial planner and of course, to tie it all together, a property advisor or mentor. In addition, you'll need builders, tradespeople, quantity surveyors, property managers, solicitors and various other advisors along the way. Before engaging them, ask about their experience, past projects and specific investment savvy.

Set up your structures. You'll see there is a huge benefit in getting this right from the beginning, not only to impress your mortgage broker but also to ensure you're managing your risk appropriately. Just don't take a leaf out of Lynne's book!

I can't stress enough how important it is to get your team in place first. Most investors bumble their way through their first purchases and live to tell the tale, but it's far better to get it right the first time than to be constantly learning from mistakes.

4

WEATHERING
MARKET SHOCKS

At the time of writing, the world is still in the grip of the unprecedented COVID-19 pandemic, with many countries experiencing varying degrees of lockdowns, infection rates, vaccinations and, tragically, deaths.

While the effects of the pandemic will be felt for years to come, the health scare is not the first shock to the housing market in recent times. Over the past few decades, many will remember the stock market crash of 1987, the recession 'we had to have' in the early 1990s, the tech bubble of 2000, September 11 and then the Global Financial Crisis (GFC). All of these shocks, from an economic perspective, were seen at the time as 'the end of the world'.

Housing market shocks don't have to be finance-related, though. A few of you may recall the locust plague in Perth many years ago. As locusts ate their way through crops, you'd think the world was going to end given the way the experts and media talked about it, and this created a snowball effect that started to impact the economy and the financial markets. Like all shocks, though, it didn't last.

People panic when there is a global, Australia-wide or state-level shock, and everyone freaks out thinking that it's going to be forever.

Even the property experts during COVID-19 thought the sky was going to fall in. But look at all these big events and what property prices did – they recovered (and then some).

In the case of the pandemic, Australia has weathered the storm brilliantly so far. At the time of writing, we have moved into a period of cautious growth from a state of recovery in the March 2021 quarter, off the back of successful government stimulus packages including JobKeeper and HomeBuilder, as well as the continued rollout – albeit slow – of COVID-19 vaccines.

> **Mentor tip**
> Look at all the big events and what property prices did –
> they recovered.

So, what did I do in 2020? I went out there and bought nine properties – six apartments, two commercial properties and a house that will be developed in the future. I thought that prices were pretty good, I could see that a lot of people were panic-selling, and I decided that if I could pick up a few good deals, I would. I also want to make it clear that I steer clear of distressed sales and property investments where I would benefit from someone's misfortunes. I'll leave that to others! It's not that I was waiting for a global pandemic, but I had enough buffers in place to take advantage of opportunities that fit my overall plan and strategy.

As the saying goes, I've been around the block a few times, and I've seen market shocks before, so I understand how things typically pan out. More importantly, I'm prepared for these situations and am ready to take advantage when the opportunity is ripe, rather than sit on the sidelines waiting to see what happens.

The long and short of it is that it's very unlikely that we will all get struck down by a 'worst-case scenario', such as a meteor hitting Earth and no-one surviving.

There has never been a better time to get into the property market or continue to grow your existing portfolio. Interest rates are at an all-time low, and the next decade looks set to remain a relatively low-interest-rate environment. Unlike the decades behind us, these low interest rates are the new normal; many investors don't know what it feels like to pay upwards of 20 per cent interest rates, as was the case during the 1980s, or even the historical interest rates averaging around 7 per cent. What comes down must come up, and vice versa! Weathering the market shocks all comes down to planning and preparation, whether the shocks are in or out of your control. And that's exactly how I position myself so that I can keep my eyes peeled on maximising opportunities. This is what I suggest...

TAKE A LAYERED APPROACH

The key is to not have all your eggs in one basket – spread them around. Also, as I have always said, don't just have eggs! If something happens to you, your tenant or your financial situation, you need some level of cover. A layered approach includes:

- A standard insurance policy for landlord protection, plus bolt-ons including lost rent, tenant default and malicious damage, depending on your policy
- Income protection, because if you lose your job, you need to be able to fall back on some income insurance
- Financial buffers. Your amount of savings is going to differ depending on your circumstances, and your comfort levels. A good rule of thumb is to work out what you think is the longest you'd be out of work for if you lost your job, and then put aside your income for that period of time.

TAKE INTO ACCOUNT THE TYPE OF PROPERTIES YOU INVEST IN

Good planning will also pay off if you own older properties, due to the higher requirement of maintenance. If you have five older properties, you're probably going to need to put a significant amount of money aside for big repairs that will inevitably be required. So, if you've got older properties, make a list of what could go wrong with each property and build the repair costs into your forecasting. If you have a portfolio that's dating a little bit, get a building inspection done at least every five years. These are preventative measures to save you money in the long run, and they can be factored in and budgeted for. Taking these measures is one of the things that differentiates a professional investor from your average investor who wings it.

Mentor tip

Preventative measures on older properties will save you money in the long run. Don't be complacent – property maintenance problems have a habit of creeping up on you!

On the other hand, new properties are more hassle-free for weathering the storms. You're getting all the tax depreciation benefits, low repairs and maintenance, and they rent well because there are no safety issues or bad smells! There's typically some level of heating and air conditioning, a dishwasher and all the amenities that tenants want. Therefore, you don't need these huge buffers in place for a rainy day if you've got insurances in place.

Mentor tip

New properties have plenty to offer investors – everything's brand new, there are great tax benefits and less risk of things falling apart when you least expect it.

THE LAST WORD

The hardest part of investing is not the buying, it's the keeping and maintaining. Interest rates will go up, governments will change and other shocks, both small and large, will come. If you're aware of what's possible and are prepared, your best defence is simply to adapt. Look at the potential risks and ensure that you have the best protections and buffers in place to ride out the shocks.

Now that you've taken the steps to get ready, you're ready to launch. Let's dive into our first batch of strategies – the easy fit.

PART II

THE
EASY

FIT

5

NEGATIVE GEARING

If there's one thing I can teach you about property, it's that slow and steady is better than fast and furious. I've always said that with investing, slow and steady wins the race. That's why I've selected these first four strategies as excellent performers if you're just starting out or seeking a solid, stable and consistent investment option straight up. These are the methodologies that are popular if you wish to add one or two properties to your portfolio – just remember that for a strategy to be a good fit, it must fit with your overall plan.

Let's kick off with one of the most hyped strategies – negative gearing.

People love to talk about negative gearing because they've heard and read about it in the papers and on television. Everyone loves to weigh in on what they think – good or bad. The problem is there are many misconceptions around positive and negative gearing, and individual opinions and arguments often represent only a small part of the story.

Let me show you an example. Some people think that properties are inherently either positively or negatively geared. Have a look at figure 5.1 on the next page, which shows side-by-side townhouses.

One of these townhouses is negatively geared. Can you tell which?

Nope – of course not! The thing is, you can't tell just by looking at the property or its location. The most important thing to wrap your head around is that positive or negative gearing is simply a tax treatment. It's not the property itself – it's the treatment of the financials and the resulting tax position. It's such a common misconception.

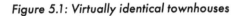

Figure 5.1: Virtually identical townhouses

> **Mentor tip**
>
> Positive and negative gearing is a tax position. It's not a property 'type'. Never forget that!

POSITIVE GEARING

Let's start with positively geared property. Typically, investors chase a cashflow return on their property that is higher than the cost of all the interest, management fees, council rates, insurances and any other outgoings they must pay. In other words, you get more back from your rental income than the cost of all your outgoings.

Many investors wrongly assume that positive cashflow properties are only found in regional areas, areas with low growth potential or in mining towns. Sometimes, it's assumed that a positively geared property is 'higher risk', and while that can be the case in some regional areas and mining towns, positively geared properties can be found everywhere.

The issue is that people chase positively geared properties with this mindset: 'I don't want property that takes money out of my pocket every week; instead, I want property that puts money into my pocket every week.' Yes, it makes sense as an investor to seek a cashflow return, and you might have money going into your pocket every week, but that amount is probably not going to be enough to retire on. Let's say a positively geared property gives you $1000 a month (and that's a lot for a typical property), which works out to be $230.77 a week. While this is rare – and we're also assuming it's *consistently* yielding $1000 a month – it's also nowhere near enough to retire on by itself. The simple truth is that most people will need quite a few properties to replace their income.

You're going to need ten of those properties to give you $120,000 income total. That's a lot of properties for most people, given that means you also need to manage ten kitchens, at least ten (and probably more like twenty) bathrooms and ten hot water systems, all needing repairs and maintenance.

A better focus is to keep the balance right between managing the cashflow outcome of the property and the capital growth of the property. Let's get real, no-one is realistically going to build wealth from a property that gives them $30 a week positive income.

NEGATIVE GEARING

A negatively geared property is simply a property that takes money from your pocket each month – so after all the expenses and income are factored in, you have a shortfall at the end of the month. You can then claim that shortfall as a tax deduction in your personal tax return – giving you a nice cashback 'bonus' – and, at the same time, increase the capital value of your property. For example, say your investment property earned $40,000 per year in rent and the claimable outgoings totalled $45,000: that means you can claim back a $5000 loss on your personal tax return.

So, why do it?

But why would you invest in something that costs you hundreds of dollars (or more) every month? Good question. Once again, it all depends on your overall strategy. Put simply, you might choose a negatively geared investment property if you expect that the value of the property, or the rent (or both), will increase over time at a rate that is greater than the loss. This is called a capital gain.

The cashflow of a property is fluid: it changes over time. So, the cashflow position of a property today will be different in two years, five years, ten years and so on. I may purchase a property today that is negatively geared, but in ten years the expenses are less than the income. I have also likely reduced the debt on the property, which has contributed to changing it to a positive cashflow position. Therefore, it has given me tax benefits the whole time I've held it, plus it has accumulated significant capital growth. And that's because it fit into my overall strategy.

So, to put it simply, negative gearing is when:

- you borrow to acquire an investment
- the interest and other costs you incur are more than the rental income you receive from the investment (in other words you make a cash loss)
- this cash loss, and non-cash deductions, are offset against income from other sources, thus reducing your taxable income and, therefore, the amount of tax you must pay (compared to the tax you'd pay without the investment).

WHAT YOU NEED TO KNOW

Any property can be made into a positively or negatively geared property, as the gearing of a property is simply a tax treatment.

This means that the depreciation benefits are an on-paper loss, not an actual loss. If you lose money on paper, you can claim it on tax, and doing so might change your tax position. As I've said before, treat it like a business, not a side gig or hobby.

Let me explain further. Property investing is a taxable activity, and just like with a business or shares, any income earned or losses made will impact your income position and the amount of tax you need to pay. A property with **negative cashflow** means the rental income from that property does not cover all the outgoing cash costs associated with that particular property. Essentially, it makes a loss. It's this loss that reduces the investor's overall tax liability.

Adding the word 'gearing' simply means that the property has been acquired using borrowed funds, and that interest on that borrowing forms part of the expenses. So, a **positively geared** property is one for which the rental income from that property is *greater* than all the outgoing cash costs, including the borrowings. Meanwhile, a **negatively geared** property is one for which the rental income from that property is *less* than all the outgoing cash costs.

You also need to understand that your property can switch to and from being negatively geared and positively geared, depending on a range of external factors. For example, in a strong market you might get a higher rent, but when that lease expires the market may have cooled a little bit, so your property might be vacant for a period or you might have to drop the rent.

Mentor tip

Keep your finger on the pulse by reading the local property news where your property is located, so you can stay updated with local market conditions. This will help in discussions with your property manager about the rental market.

To make matters more confusing, a 'negatively geared' property can have positive cashflow on paper, but only after income tax considerations have been considered – that is, after you have taken tax credits gained from legitimate tax deductions into account. These can include that 'negative cashflow' and 'non-cash' deductions such as the depreciation of the building as well as the fixtures and fittings, which will vary from one property to the next.

Mentor tip

Chasing positive cashflow properties could be like getting a window seat on the *Titanic* – it's great for a while but eventually it won't matter when you run into other problems.

You can see this in figure 5.2. Essentially, the cashflow position is determined before tax, but the gearing of the property is determined after tax. In the below example, the raw numbers of the property before any tax considerations show that the property is in the red and costing the investor money. This means the property is producing a negative cashflow. However, after everything goes 'in the wash' and the tax position is calculated, the property is in positive cashflow territory. Making a decision on the raw numbers alone could potentially cost you in the long run, which is why you need a great team around you to guide you.

Figure 5.2: Negative versus positive cashflow and gearing

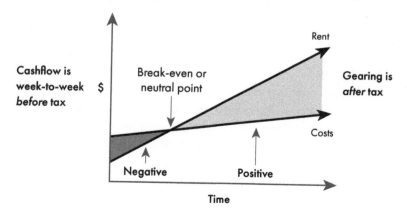

So, it is possible for a property to be *negative* cashflow but *positively* geared.

A TALE OF TWO INVESTORS

Consider this: Investor A buys a property for $500,000. She puts down a 10 per cent deposit and has a $450,000 loan. After all expenses, she still needs to contribute $50 per week out of pocket, making this property negatively geared.

Investor B buys a property for $500,000. He puts down a 20 per cent deposit and has a $400,000 loan. After all expenses, because the loan amount is less, the property produces a return of $50 per week, making this property positively geared.

Of course, this is an overly simplified example, but you can see how the gearing outcome can be completely different on identical properties. Both properties have the same potential to provide tax depreciation benefits and will rent well for the investors, but due to the deposits invested into each property, the loan amounts are different. Also, because the investors are borrowing different amounts, they will have different tax positions.

Looking to the future, let's assume they earn the same amounts and each had access to $100,000 for deposits. Investor A only spent $50,000 on a deposit for her property, so she now has another deposit sitting there that could be used to secure another property in the marketplace. So, while Investor A may be out of pocket $50 per week to hold her first property, she now has access to another deposit which could be used to secure another property.

As for Investor B, he has some extra income coming in with the extra $50 a week. It's handy, but it's probably not enough to replace his income. This investor must declare this income in his tax return and, of course, he will need to pay tax on that. And he has nothing left for another deposit.

While these are just raw numbers and the tax depreciation benefits have not been included in this basic scenario, you can start to get the picture.

Two different approaches

In this example, both investors with the same income and the same amount for deposits can create two totally different property portfolios. If Investor A was able to service that second loan and use her spare $50,000 on another property, she'd have $1,000,000 in the marketplace working for her. Investor B wanted positive cashflow, so he put down a bigger deposit, but he only has $500,000 in the marketplace.

Let's look at them side by side in table 5.1, assuming a 5 per cent capital growth rate.

Table 5.1: Comparing two different investment approaches

	Investor A	Investor B
Portfolio value	$1,000,000	$500,000
Debt position	$900,000	$400,000
Cashflow	-$100 per week	+$50 per week
10-year growth	$1,628,894	$814,447
Equity	$728,894	$314,447
Cashflow adjustment	-$52,000 over 10 years	+$26,000 over 10 years
Net position	$676,894	$340,447

We can see that Investor A is a whopping **$336,447** better off just by tweaking her strategy and securing a second property.

Investor A may have had to make a few sacrifices to hold her two properties: she may have had to dine out a little less, maybe make coffee at home instead of buying it from a café every day, or spent less on other areas. But *most* people on an average income could find an extra $50 to $100 a week if they really had to. And yes, a lot of people reading this might scoff at that and say, 'You've got to be kidding me, Luke,' but I know it's true because if the goal is big enough, you will find a way. This doesn't mean stretching yourself to the eyeballs but just managing your spending and being a better money manager. I've always said to myself, 'How can I make this happen?' rather than, 'Oh, I can't afford that,' or, 'This will never work.'

Some of the properties that have cost me money out of pocket and been negatively geared have gone on to perform extremely well. Having a negatively geared property in the right area as part of a clear strategy can be a great move, so it shouldn't be ruled out. In the right capital growth areas, you will build wealth faster than with a positive cashflow property giving you $50 per week (which you'll still need to pay tax on).

THE POSITIVE CASHFLOW UNICORN PROPERTY

In the 2000s, there were some Australian mining towns that were attractive to investors – specifically in Western Australia and Queensland. But I could see people were paying astronomical prices for some of them, and that this was unsustainable.

For example, properties in the Wild West (Western Australia) – and some very average looking ones at that – were selling for well over $1 million and renting at $1500 per week. I had many conversations with 'savvy investors' who told me (often quite smugly) that they knew what they were doing, that mining was going to continue forever and that they would be OK.

The sad news is that a lot of investors ended up with mortgages that sent them broke when the mining boom ended. Property prices halved and rents crashed. Many people got burnt, and it no doubt crippled many people financially – some irreparably.

The take-home message is that these were unicorn properties – so-called 'can't-lose' properties apparently set to yield insane cashflow and capital growth. As I wrote earlier, unicorn properties don't exist. They're bright, shiny objects that are too good to be true. Yes, properties like this can bring a lot of money into an area, but ultimately, investing in positive cashflow areas because they're tipped as 'boom' areas, or because they're already 'booming', is a fool's game. This is not investing in my opinion – it's gambling. To be successful, you must know when to get in and when to get out (in the wise words of Kenny Rogers), and even then, there's no real strategy behind that. It's more like blind luck than anything else. Exercise extreme caution with these types of properties!

The truth is, as I've said before, the unsexy, boring properties are those that work best in most cases. If you want your trophy home, build your wealth first, get that passive income for life, and then go and buy your trophy. Build your portfolio with the boring stuff first.

Case study

Referring back to my third purchase from Chapter 1, when I was 24 I bought a property in Queenstown, Tasmania. I'd bought it after reading Steve McKnight's book *From 0 to 130 Properties in 3.5 Years*. Great, I said to myself. This was what I needed to make all my dreams come true. The problem was that when the book came out, prices were on the move in Bendigo and Ballarat and, not surprisingly, the best time to buy in those areas was precisely two-and-a-half years earlier – when Steve bought! (Bugger.) So, given that I couldn't afford them, I started scouring the internet for other areas that could give me this golden goose property.

Not long after, I found one: a $79,500 property in Queenstown, Tasmania, rented for $120 per week. What a bargain! I had a positive cashflow property! Now I just had to sit back and wait for the cash to start rolling in, right? With that sorted, I went on my merry way, satisfied I'd bought my third property purchase in under four years, forgetting such trivial details as repairs and maintenance, rates, insurance and property management fees. I was quite chuffed with myself.

Not long after, the heater went. That was $1200, noting of course that it frequently gets to zero degrees in winter in Queenstown, so you need a high-quality heater to keep your tenant warm. After that, a small storm blew half the fence down. Given the block size was around 1200 m², that cost me $2000 to replace. A year or two later, a new hot water system was needed ($1500); the tenant damaged the walls, so they needed repainting ($4000); the gutters needed repairs ($600); and there were various plumbing issues ($1000+). There were also the property management costs, which were more expensive to offset the low rents: 11 per cent plus GST. On top of that, council rates were just under $2000 per annum. That's a lot of outgoings and expenses for a property that only generated a little over $6000 per year.

It didn't take long before my amazing positive cashflow property became a charity case that really gave me no benefit. I was supporting the tenant by providing a roof over their head, and I was supporting the local tradies with all the ongoing repairs and maintenance, and of course, I was supporting the property management business, too. But the net result was that the property neither made me money nor lost me money in the end. I sold it a few years ago because there was virtually no capital growth or growth potential, and it was basically a

> lesson learnt. While I wouldn't call it a bad experience or a dud property, it certainly didn't break any records, and it did free up some cash for me to do something better with.

POSITIVE OR NEGATIVE?

To determine whether you should be looking for negatively geared or positively geared property, you need to run the numbers and have a clear understanding of what that property is going to do for you. Again, it all comes back to your strategy.

Time and time again, I see people oversimplifying the process by saying they want to buy a property that must be positively geared, or that must provide capital growth, but that's it. No timeline to hold or sell, and no clear outcome. When I buy property, one of the first things I know upfront even before I start looking is exactly what I want that property to do for me. What that means is that every property I add to my portfolio must have a specific purpose and must fit in with the rest of the portfolio properties. If it doesn't have a specific purpose, then I won't buy it. It's like a piece of a jigsaw puzzle: it looks nice and is close enough to fit the others, and you might even be able to make it fit if you force it, but it's not supposed to be there. Forcing something into your property portfolio when it clearly doesn't fit is going to cost you time and money.

Below, I summarise the three positive and negative reasons for each strategy.

TOP 3 POSITIVES AND NEGATIVES

Positive gearing

Positives

1. Surplus income over and above all expenses to allow the investor a buffer over and above the outgoings.

2. Less stress having to worry about finding extra cash, meaning that the property will essentially pay its own bills plus some.

3. May assist with borrowing for more property, as lenders will see that the cashflow position exceeds the expenses.

Negatives

1. Often investors will choose property based on its cashflow outcome rather than its investment fundamentals and may not end up with the best long-term investment.

2. A positively geared property may not remain that way as interest rates, repairs and other expenses affect the cashflow position. To add to this, the investor's position can (and likely will) change over time.

3. Investors focusing on investing purely on 'positive cashflow' may be missing out on some excellent opportunities to build a solid portfolio. After all, it comes down to selecting the right properties for your long-term goals.

Negative gearing

Positives

1. Significant tax advantages for buying an investment property, allowing property investors to save on tax yet still hold an asset.

2. Lenders are often able to 'add back' some of these on-paper losses to their loan-servicing calculators, so you may continue to borrow despite having a loss.

3. Short-term negative gearing is frequently offset by capital growth if the asset is held long enough.

Negatives

1. Cashflow drain can kill an otherwise healthy portfolio. Investors with an already negatively geared property are more sensitive to interest-rate rises and other costs.

2. Investors relying on negative gearing could be affected if the tax laws change. While this is not likely in the near term, there is some (small) risk that policy could change at some point or be 'tweaked' by the government of the day.

3. The first rule of negative gearing is, 'You don't speak about negative gearing'. Just like in *Fight Club*, it's best to keep this to yourself. Mention negative gearing to anyone and you're likely going to be seen as a 'greedy landlord' or someone who's 'ripping off the other taxpayers'. Again, this comes back to other people's misunderstanding of what it is and can create unnecessary debates with people you otherwise like. Essentially, negative gearing is something that you should probably discuss in the privacy of your own home!

THE LAST WORD

Make sure you know the specific purpose of each property in your portfolio before you start looking for it. To do that, you need a road map of what your end goal is and how that looks; after all, how can you put your puzzle together if you don't know what the end picture is supposed to look like? At the end of the day, negative gearing is not for everyone. However, under current legislation, there are taxation benefits that could assist you to build your portfolio faster. So, negative gearing is just one tool out of many available to help you get ahead.

6

ESTABLISHED RESIDENTIAL PROPERTY

Established residential property is often the 'go to' property investment. Why? Because people love to drive around and look at properties in person. You can touch and feel bricks and mortar, and it can seem safer and more feasible than other, more speculative strategies.

As a result, many investors start off their property portfolios this way accidentally, because they simply 'liked' a property. Now, this is a very basic entry into investing, and it can certainly work if you know what you're doing. In saying that, skydiving works too if you know what you're doing.

BRICKS AND MORTAR

One of the benefits of established residential property is that you can see it, walk through it and, to a certain extent, know what you're buying. You can have a building inspection and a pest report completed with relative ease and know upfront if there are any problems. Furthermore, there is often a history of tenants in established residential property, so you can work with exact figures to calculate the potential investment results.

When comparing established properties, it can be extremely difficult to work out where to begin. I mean, there are thousands of suburbs across each state, let alone the country – so, how do you start comparing, especially when you're unfamiliar with the territory?

Firstly, you need to take a step back. What's your intent for the property? Is it to buy and leave as is, renovate or develop, or do a quick tidy up and then flip it? Once you know how buying established property fits in with your overall plan, then you can narrow it down to what its purpose will be.

Secondly, there are a few fundamental things to look out for when it comes to established residential property. Generally, these apply to all properties, but for existing residential property in this category, you'll need to understand what is going to make *that particular property in that area increase in value and rental income* over time.

Start off by making a list of the fundamental factors that will provide growth, such as:

- What type of tenant will want to live there?
- Is this a family orientated area, or is it better for students or young professionals?
- Will the tenant spend most of their time *in* the property or *out* of the property?

GOLDEN RULES

I'd like to share my golden rules around investing in established residential property.

Defects

The first rule is to ensure there are no structural defects. This is a basic one; make sure that the thing is not falling down. Why? Because it could cost you an absolute fortune to fix it up. For example, if you see something online in a good area for much less than anything else listed, that's probably because no-one wants it. That's why it's listed online. Usually, these types of properties are presented to builders first, and then if they end up online it's because they're going to cost a huge amount of money to fix up. By the time you spend that money, you've also lost time, and experienced the headaches that go with it. You'll probably end up spending the same money as buying at a higher price point. So, why not just spend that upfront and avoid the headaches?

The other thing to note is that if there are structural defects, the banks won't lend on the property – or if they do, they'll often lend only on land value. And the house would have to be knocked down before they'd lend on just the land only, as they see the structurally defective house as a risk to the land.

Location

One of the biggest mistakes I see is when people buy property close to where they live. It feels safe because you know the area, and what you're buying feels well known, too. But beware – how does it fit in with your bigger plan? How do you know it will deliver the returns that you are anticipating? Where does it fit in with your next purchase, and the one after that?

Look at the fundamentals. Is the property close to shops, schools and public transport? Know your market, and know your competition, so that you can make sure you're getting the best deal.

Agents

As you know, not all agents are created equal. There are ethical agents out there, and there are unethical agents out there too. You'd hope it's at least 80 per cent who are ethical and 20 per cent who are not, but that could be flipped around depending on which market and suburb you're in.

Then, there's the game you have to play. When you buy established properties, you don't necessarily have transparency around what's really going on. Keep in mind that all agents act for the vendor, so they don't have your best interests at heart; also, in the majority of cases, they are not trained in property investment fundamentals.

Agents are out there to try and get the best price and the best deal for their vendors. You generally never know the story behind the scenes; this is a good reason why most of the best properties don't appear on the popular real estate sales websites.

Let me explain. If you're a really good real estate agent and you have a property that you know is a good deal in a good area, what's the first thing you're going to do? You're going to ring your friends, family and favorite people in your network, such as developers or customers in the area who buy lots of property. They may already have ten properties on your rent roll, which makes them a good bet for further income for your agency. Online listing companies are often the *last* step for agents rather than the first step. Why pay to advertise if you don't need to?

Competition

With established property, there's a bit more groundwork to do to make sure you're getting a good deal. You need to know your market and your competition, and especially who else is buying property. Are you going to up be against investors? Developers? Owner occupiers or builders?

If you're buying a site for development, you'll be competing with builders. And builders don't need a development margin, they just need their build margin. (See 'Beating the competition' on page 144 for a detailed explanation of this.) So, they'll pay the gap between the price and your development margin because they're just going to get their build margin. If you try to compete with that, you'll make no money, or at the very least it will be harder for you to make a profit.

Tax implications

To date in Australia, income tax and capital gains tax changes haven't been retrospective, and existing investors have been protected from the impact of changes. For instance, all property assets purchased before 19 September 1985 are exempt from capital gains tax, and only assets purchased after that date are subject to the current tax provisions.

In 2018, the rules changed around the tax benefits that can be claimed on established property, wiping out a lot of the deductions that had been available.

Mentor tip

When buying existing residential property, consider the tax benefits and discuss with your accountant first to make sure you understand what you can and can't claim.

BUYER BEWARE

Established properties can slow down your investing, too. I know this because it happened to me. Imagine you've settled on a property that's 20 to 30 years old, and the rent is starting to come in. All good. You've started to plan your next property purchase. You're saving like crazy, putting away $100 a week, and even though it may take a while, you have big goals and are planning on being diligent so you can get your next property deposit together. Then, the emails roll in from your property manager about some 'problems' starting to appear, and suddenly your hard-earned income is eaten up by maintenance bills.

Case study

This is a simplified version of what happened on one of my properties many years ago.

'Hi Luke, the tenants have reported a leak coming into the property and would like to get someone out to inspect it.'

OK, no worries. After organising a plumber to attend and do some patch-up work to the roof, another message appeared a week later.

'Hi Luke, the leak has returned, and the tenants are reporting that the carpet in one of the bedrooms is soaking wet. I have arranged for the plumber to attend again to see if they can find out what it is, but there is mould starting to form in the bedroom, so one of their kids is now sleeping the lounge room. We will need to get someone out to attend to the mould. Can you please confirm this is OK?'

This was followed a few weeks later by another message.

'Hi Luke, we have just had written confirmation from the tenant that the mould has gotten worse, and they have had an air quality test done. The test shows the property is uninhabitable, and they have advised they are going to move out and break the lease.'

Not sure I signed up for this! Not only did I have a significant amount to pay in bills for repairs and maintenance, but I also lost rent and had an insurance claim to deal with. But I had to deal with it, and now this property is working out beautifully, with no leaking – but it would have been nice to avoid all that in the first place!

BUILDING REPORTS

When things go wrong – and they will – it can be a hard pill to swallow. With established property, you *must* expect that things will go wrong. A property may have been beautifully renovated, but there could still be hidden problems that have simply been patched over. What you need to keep in mind is that landlord and building insurance often won't cover you for many of these expenses. You'll also need to pay for the initial callouts for the plumber, the reimbursement of the tenants' costs to obtain reports, and lost rent, which usually has minimum waiting periods. Basically, the old saying *caveat emptor* (buyer beware) applies here.

You can get all the building reports you like before you buy, but at the end of the day you will find that almost *all* these reports will have clauses in them that specifically state that the report they are doing for you is a visual inspection only. This means there is a limit to how much was inspected, and you need to be aware that a visual inspection will never be able to pick up everything that could go wrong. While a building report on an existing residential property is still a good idea, I would assume that the report would realistically only cover around 30 to 40 per cent (at best) of things that could go wrong with the property, so you will need to do your own research over and above the building report and know what to look out for. Property managers and lawyers I work with tell me that 'mould is the new asbestos' these days, so keep a close eye out for any water leaks or mould.

Mentor tip

If you're considering established residential property, don't just look for the cheapest one out there. Make sure you get a thorough building inspection and pest report done, and make sure you're aware of what is and isn't included in the reports. For example, some building inspections exclude plumbing and electrical, and others exclude inspecting under the house or in the roof cavity. Basically, the more thorough the better.

It's also worth mentioning that when you receive your completed building report, it can sound negative. But it must! Can you imagine a building report that came back saying, 'All good, there's nothing wrong with it, nothing to look out for, it's perfect and you should buy it'? I've never had a building inspection report returned that said any words to that effect; every one of them, without exception, has found fault with the building. And they all sound terrible. Many of them have been, but for good reason, and I haven't proceeded with those purchases.

Often these comments are just 'for your information' and nothing to panic about. For example, the report might make a comment on the hot water system: 'The hot water system is 16 years old, has rust around the brackets and there are a few signs of water leaks, and the cover is badly worn.' When you read it, you might be inclined to think that it's falling apart, but at the end of the day hot water systems do have a lifespan – they don't last forever. So, seeing something like this on a report is not there to scare you, but simply to state that the appliance is nearing the end of its usable life and will need to be replaced sometime soon. It might last another week or two, or it could kick on for another five years.

NEED TO KNOW

In 2020, the Victorian government announced big changes to the *Residential Tenancies Act*. Reforms have been in the works since 2017 but were delayed due to COVID-19, finally coming into effect on 29 March 2021. Essentially, there's more risk for older properties moving forward, with the upshot that the standards are being lifted for rental accommodation.

This means that if you're holding an established property, it may cost you more on compliance as well as to meet tenant demands. There will be more inspections and requirements around electrical safety. For example, smoke detectors must be tested every 12 months. The electrical and plumbing also must be certified every two years, to make sure that everything's compliant to a high standard.

There are changes to payment breaches, too. For example, if there is something that's unsafe in the property and the tenant reports it, but the report is not acted upon, the fines have increased. Also, a tenant can be 14 days late to pay the rent four times in a 12-month period and it won't affect their rent record, and you can't issue a notice to vacate.

I think these new changes reflect a general cultural movement in which more people are renting these days. And not only that, people are renting for longer, too. So, there's a whole generation of people growing up who have no intention of buying a property – ever. We will become a renter's nation over the next 20 to 30 years, just like many European nations. Tenants want to live in properties that have nice carpet, a nice kitchen and nice bathrooms, and are of a higher quality than what people have expected previously.

If you have an older property, you'll be competing with more and more newer properties as our capital cities consolidate and stop sprawling out at the fringes. We have been spreading out over the last 50 years, and now governments at all levels are waking up to the idea of having more compact cities and are planning infrastructure this way, too. Landlords are going to be buying newer properties because they're going to be more compliant. They can also rent for more because tenants will pay a small premium to live in something nicer – or that has taps that don't leak and showers that are water efficient, for example. Because of this, older properties are going to struggle to capture that rental market.

Mentor tip

The federal government is supporting new construction and investing in new infrastructure to provide jobs and encourage money to flow through the economy. They're disincentivising buying older properties by reducing tax benefits, and the compliance side of things has now stepped up.

TOP 3 POSITIVES AND NEGATIVES

Positives

1. You know exactly what you're getting. An obvious positive here is that you can see and touch (and sometimes smell!) the property before purchasing.

2. Established housing can often be improved to add value, such as through renovation, subdivision or further development.

3. Usually, second-hand property can be bought, settled and tenanted relatively quickly, so if it's on the market you can buy it and not have to wait.

Negatives

1. Buying a second-, third- or fourth- (or more) hand property means that you could be buying a building that has had many patch-ups or repairs – often performed over many years – or has hidden and sometimes costly faults. Building reports are good but often do not include structural defects.

2. Ongoing repairs and maintenance can affect your cashflow and slow down your property portfolio growth. If you need to divert funds towards repairs and maintenance, it could slow you down from adding your next property to your portfolio. The long-term compounding costs of that can be *huge*.

3. Often tax depreciation benefits are massively reduced or non-existent for these types of properties. Together, the lack of tax benefits and the repair bills can cause a big hit to your financials.

THE LAST WORD

Buying a 'property for investment' is very different to being a serious, professional property investor. Sure, the process of acquiring a property for investment technically makes someone a property investor; however, to get the best results, you need to invest like a business. My suggestion would be that if you're looking at an older property, first be aware of the tenancy laws, especially if it's a very old property. Companies that are currently doing building inspections will then probably bolt on a safety inspection as well to assist with this compliance. Make sure you have some extra money tucked away for repairs and maintenance, over and above your regular buffer amount.

7

NEW OR OFF-THE-PLAN RESIDENTIAL PROPERTY

New and off-the-plan residential properties tick a lot of boxes when it comes to investing for the long-term. New properties can be completed houses, townhouses, villas or apartments that have been released by a developer at the completion of a project. Often developers will hold on to some of their properties to sell once completed, expecting to capitalise on higher prices. Retail purchasers often prefer to see a finished product, and as such, this can attract a premium on the sale price for developers.

Buying off the plan provides benefits to purchasers, developers and builders. Purchasers may be able to get in first and secure one of the better properties in a development, among other incentives. Developers are keen to secure presales in their projects as this is often the 'trigger' for their commercial funding to build the project. Without these presales, the development may not get off the ground in most cases. If off-the-plan properties are bought well, smart investors can benefit from some growth in the property before it's completed.

THE STRATEGY

The strategy behind buying new or off-the-plan property will be different for each investor. However, one of the main reasons most people pursue this strategy is the significant tax benefits.

Given the federal government changes to depreciation benefits that came into effect in 2018, investors buying new properties now have the upper hand when it comes to claiming the most from their property. Conversely, many investors buying established property will miss out on the tax savings associated with new properties. Savvy investors use this strategy to help them to build their portfolios faster, which leads to better cashflow and better tax benefits.

Basically, the main tax benefits that you can claim deductions on are new plant and equipment (also known as the fixtures and fittings) as well as the actual building itself. The building depreciation is typically done over a 40-year period and includes the floor, walls, roof and anything 'structural'. Anything stuck to the building, such as carpets, air conditioners, kitchens, bathrooms and even electrical wiring and light switches, is deemed to have a much shorter lifespan.

Another benefit of buying new properties is that they come with a warranty. It varies in every state, but typically a new building will have a six- to ten-year warranty on any major structural defects. Then, the ease with which you can make a claim on that warranty depends on the builder or developer. If you're purchasing from a reputable developer, they will have an interest in protecting their brand and their identity in the marketplace.

However, in every property cycle, you will see new developers pop up and build, and it can be difficult to claim on the warranty because they're not necessarily reputable. In all cases, it pays to do your research and obtain good legal advice upfront before signing anything.

The benefits of having a new build with a builder's warranty are many. While most new properties have no issues, it provides great peace of mind to know that you have some protection, especially for structural defects. An older property won't have this level of protection, so aside from all the other benefits of new property, knowing the building itself is sound really is helpful.

When buying new or off the plan, it always pays to do your research and understand the developer's track record. When you understand who is behind the project and learn their history of success or failure, you'll be much better informed if you choose to move forward with them. Sometimes this information is not readily available, so it helps to dig a little deeper to find out the history of the development company and the directors. While a lot of development projects are marketed under a parent developer, it's common for developers to do a project in a special purpose vehicle (SPV), which is a company set up just for that project. You can learn more about SPVs in Chapter 11. As a strategy, a bright and shiny new property offers great opportunities both in the flesh and on paper. New residential property may be under construction due to redevelopment in the area, because it's close to new infrastructure or because the area is ready to take off. You'll be in the box seat for when property prices start increasing.

Mentor tip

Developers and builders get a bad rap in the media, some for good reason. Do your due diligence and look up their credentials. A great place to start is if they have a professional company website. However, it's worth mentioning that smaller development projects are often done 'off market' and don't necessarily have (or even need) flashy brochures or websites to sell their stock.

HOTSPOTS

Is chasing the latest hotspot the key to success? There are advanced software platforms available that claim to 'pick' – or assist with selecting – the next hotspot. You barely have to lift a finger for this, and of course, it can be done from the comfort of your own home. But keep in mind that these software platforms are simply crunching data. They do not factor in your own personal circumstances, goals or specific desired outcomes, and they rarely factor in the big picture. I've seen people spend literally thousands of dollars on software platforms that claim to pinpoint the very best property to buy. However, when there's only data to consider and not the investor's personal situation, it can be very risky to rely on this alone. Furthermore, the areas don't always fit your price point or cashflow outcomes. They may forecast a spectacular growth opportunity with low days on market, shortage of supply and rents and prices increasing; however, this may just be an anomaly – a one-time spike in a local market and no guarantee of long-term results.

This means you could be making an important investment decision based on data that is simply a snapshot in time, rather than on key fundamentals. At the same time, a one-time discount to the market or a special deal could come from local knowledge that isn't readily available on these platforms. So, before making your purchasing decision, make sure you've done your homework.

Mentor tip

If it sounds too good to be true, it probably is. Plan, do your homework, and then base your decisions on sound market data and statistics. Think long term.

NEW RESIDENTIAL PROPERTY

When it comes to new properties, let's return to the key point – your investing strategy is just as important as the property itself. Refer back to the first few chapters of this book! Now, new residential property is essentially any brand-new building that has just been completed and has never been lived in before. After the property has had a tenant or owner-occupier in it, the property officially becomes second-hand; so, if you're looking for a new property to get the maximum tax benefits that go with it, make sure that you're buying a property that has never been occupied before.

Of course, new residential property could be a house-and-land package, a duplex, a townhouse or an apartment. As mentioned earlier, any residential property could be sold as a finished product to secure a higher price. However, there are many instances where a buyer has bought off the plan and decided to walk away from their contractual obligations (and quite often their 10 per cent deposit) and not settle on the property. This means that developers are unexpectedly left with a finished property to sell; this happened a lot during the COVID-19 crisis of 2020.

If you know where to look, who to contact and how to negotiate on these, you may be able to access some or all the previous purchaser's deposit. Not all developers are receptive to this, but at the end of the day, they're looking to sell their projects either off the plan or on completion, so there could be opportunities to secure some great assets.

Now, I know many readers are going to be wondering: what about location? What about the property itself? What if it's no good? What if I don't like the floor plan? The short answer is to focus on the numbers. Don't get too emotionally attached to the property itself, as tenants are always looking for new properties and will often pay a premium to rent one.

Mentor tip
Don't get too emotionally attached to the property itself.
Focus on the numbers.

The problem is that people often base their decision on the property alone, which means 100 per cent of that decision is based on a 'feeling' as to how the property is going to perform. A good feeling might give you some warm and fuzzies, but the reality of cold hard cash disappearing from your coffers will give you a wake-up call that will make you wish you had gone for informed due diligence.

I've met many investors holding several properties, and when I ask them how they selected them, what do you think they say? 'Well, at the time we heard this was going to be a good area, so we did some research and decided this would be a good fit for us.'

While this is how many investors add properties to their portfolios, it might start ringing some alarm bells. I did it that way too when I was starting out, and it's not the end of the world if you build a portfolio like that. But moving forward, ensure all your investment decisions are based around the property *and* the strategy, and weighing up both to make the decision. Adding new properties to your investment portfolio might just give you that boost you need to improve your tax situation, achieve a higher rental return and have happier tenants who enjoy all the modern conveniences. Tenants in newer properties are likely to stay longer, too!

> **Mentor tip**
> There are 100-plus things to consider when buying a property. How you weigh each of these things is very important. While each factor plays a part in helping you make a good investment decision, knowing how to weight each factor is the key to success.

OFF THE PLAN

Let's be honest, buying off the plan cops a bit of flak in the media. The newspapers and online publications often feature stories about 'dodgy' off-the-plan developments, and you only have to look around the inner-city suburbs in Australia to see these new developments – for better or for worse – taking up prime real estate space. But the ones seen in the media are the worst cases, because these make for the best stories. The thing to consider here (which we all seem to forget) is that at some point in time, every property you see, in every state and in every suburb, was once a new property. Someone bought that property 'new' or off the plan. So, buying new or off-the-plan property certainly isn't anything to be worried about. In fact, some of the best new properties will be snapped up before they are completed, so by disregarding off-the-plan properties as an option, you could be missing out on the best properties available.

Mentor tip

This is a solid strategy because it provides an upside for investors wanting to fast-track their portfolio, without as much fuss. In other words, new property and off-the-plan property can rent for a higher price, have fewer repairs and maintenance requirements, come with a warranty and provide excellent tax depreciation benefits – this is a great combination of factors to consider for any investor looking to build a portfolio of multiple properties!

A FUTURE OF INVESTMENT OPPORTUNITY

Here's some food for thought: with more and more people renting these days, tenants are becoming fussier about where they live. As I suggested in the previous chapter, in the years ahead, I believe there will be a wave of people who will leave school and rent *for life*. In fact, in the 2020s and beyond, we can see that it is already becoming more normal to rent, and it certainly won't have the stigma attached to it that it used to.

This is a huge shift in the Australian market and psyche. In Europe, it's rarer to own property, with most residents who live in cities opting to rent, largely due to the exorbitant costs associated with buying. I believe Australia is going the same way. In the *2015–16 Survey of Income and Housing*, it was found that an estimated 30 per cent of households owned their homes outright (that is, without a mortgage) and 37 per cent were owners with a mortgage. A further 25 per cent were renting from a private landlord and 4 per cent were renting from a state or territory housing authority.

The Great Australian Dream of a quarter-acre block and a Hills Hoist in the backyard is slowly disappearing. In its place, new residential townhouses and apartments are popping up to cope with the extra demands of population and a lack of available land to build upon – especially in the eastern-state cities. Australia's big four cities – Sydney, Melbourne, Brisbane and Perth – have grown substantially over the last 20 years, and over this time, state governments have struggled to keep up with seemingly never-ending infrastructure demands on the city fringes.

This has meant that state and local governments have had to do more with less, which has translated to higher-density construction within the existing city boundaries. While this consolidation of land in our cities does cause issues with NIMBYs (Not In My Backyard!) who will forever oppose any change and redevelopment, it is required to ensure that infrastructure in existing areas is maintained, expanded and improved over time instead of us forever building new freeways, hospitals and schools in the city fringes. As a society, it makes sense for us to use our resources more wisely and operate more efficiently. In my view, as a young country, we have been spoilt for decades, with many of us growing up in a house on a block of land. (How's the serenity?!)

What this signifies is a massive opportunity for savvy investors seeking to capitalise over the next decade and beyond. Those who understand this shift in the market and the opportunities it presents will be able to capitalise on this by planning for the future. Think about it: if tenants are looking to rent for longer periods, they will prioritise the creature comforts that owner-occupiers enjoy. That means good-quality heating and air conditioning, dishwashers, stone benchtops, quality carpets and floor coverings, and showers, toilets and taps that don't leak. Also, councils are placing tougher and tougher requirements on developers with regard to energy efficiency, and with a more environmentally conscious tenant base nowadays, this is playing a big part in tenant property selection. New properties provide all of this.

While this may seem like a pretty simple wish list, older properties that need ongoing repairs and maintenance can cause inconvenience and frustration for tenants – even though the rent may be lower. Gone are the days of rentals with old yellow carpets, walls that haven't been painted for 20-plus years and outdated kitchens and bathrooms. Those properties eventually end up dropping their rents so low that they either need a significant cash injection and full-scale renovation or are sold off to developers who will knock them down.

While there will always be a market for these types of properties, the ones that will be in demand in the next decade and beyond will be those well-located properties that have the built-in 'luxuries' now expected by the younger generation. These luxuries were often part of their childhood, in their baby-boomer parents' homes. On a global scale, Australian baby boomers have done pretty well for themselves, so their kids – an entire generation (myself included!) – have been pretty spoiled with their living standards.

You've probably seen the ads for these developments in the papers while polishing off your smashed avocado and eggs. The quality of amenities now being included in buildings is incredible – day spas, wine cellars, home theatres and workstations, as well as infinity-edge rooftop swimming pools and luxurious lounges with designer furniture all put together by big-name architects. Buyers want these lifestyle amenities while still being close to transport, so this shift in tenant demand is likely to see new properties perform well in the next decade or so as more owner-occupiers opt into the Insta-worthy lifestyles that these types of properties provide.

TOP 3 POSITIVES AND NEGATIVES

Positives

1. An obvious positive is the incredible tax savings that can be claimed on a new property. This can help you to fast-track your portfolio and get your next property sooner.

2. Tenants want newer property. Typically, new developments are attractive to tenants as they offer a better quality of life and 'creature comforts' such as air-conditioning and heating that actually works!

3. New or off-the-plan properties typically won't require any significant repairs or maintenance for the first 10 to 15 years. This allows you to direct your funds towards building your portfolio, instead of dumping it into maintaining an older property.

Negatives

1. You may need to wait. Sometimes, off-the-plan properties can be delayed, and that needs to be factored in. However, buying through a trusted source can help to minimise this risk.

2. Valuations can come in below the purchase price at settlement. This means that between the time of buying and settlement of the property, you may need to chip in some more money to complete settlement. This is particularly common in areas that are oversupplied, or in high-rise buildings.

3. You need a good lawyer. Off-the-plan contracts aren't normal property contracts, so you need a legal professional who knows how to look out for issues. As I've outlined, knowing how to find a good legal representative to protect your interests is extremely important.

THE LAST WORD

In the years ahead, buying new will appeal to more and more investors. As affordability becomes an even bigger problem, investors will find themselves in a great position to climb up the property ladder due to the tax benefits alone. Governments know that the building industry provides jobs, and a healthy property market gives people the confidence to go out there and spend money in the economy. All of this means that governments stay in power! I see the 'rent-for-life' shift as an exciting move for the property industry, and one that savvy investors can get on board with. As cities consolidate and technology becomes more and more ingrained in our lives, the 'smart cities' are those that will fit more people into less space while maintaining a high quality of life for residents. It's going to be challenging, but I feel that Australia is well placed to do this, and do it well, and property investors who take note of this trend and invest accordingly have an incredible opportunity to be part of this shift.

8

COMMERCIAL PROPERTY

It's not as sexy as residential property, but commercial property is still one of my favourite investment strategies. OK, maybe it's a little bit sexy telling someone you own a bunch of factories, or a whole office floor or three. I mean, industrial estates, factories, warehouses and offices don't have quite the same ring as heritage listings, architectural detail and high-end materiality, but that's OK. In commercial property, as with all investments, it's all about the numbers.

It's just that with commercial property, the numbers work a little differently to residential property numbers. While both are classified as 'properties', how you invest in them is worlds apart. How you buy them, how you finance them, how you lease them – it's all different. It's not romantic, and you need to take a relatively hard-nosed approach when dealing with commercial properties – even more so than with residential investing. It's a cold, hard numbers game, but, if done well, it can translate to some pretty healthy dollar signs.

WHAT IS A COMMERCIAL PROPERTY?

Commercial property can be anything from a small factory or storage unit (often referred to as a 'man cave') to a shop, childcare centre, petrol station or warehouse. Other types of commercial properties include offices, motels, supermarkets, hotels and even entire shopping centres – and the list goes on. There are many different strategies that can be overlayed on top of buying commercial property. As with residential property, there are good, bad and ugly parts to be aware of; but it really is a world away from residential investing.

Property investors who buy commercial property are typically in it for the long haul and enjoy the stability of a commercial tenancy. However, as we have all seen with COVID-19, there have been shifts in the way people work, where they work and even when they work. So, there have been a lot of commercial property owners who have been severely affected by COVID-19. Some have had to renegotiate their tenancy arrangements, and some have lost tenants altogether, especially those premises that were tenanted by small and medium-sized enterprises (SMEs).

WHY IS COMMERCIAL PROPERTY SUCH AN UNTAPPED ASSET CLASS?

At The Property Mentors, we often work with people who love the idea of owning commercial property assets or adding them to their portfolio to 'balance things out'. But understanding how, and if, these properties fit into your overall strategy is imperative if you want to add a commercial property to your portfolio. Unlike residential property, timing is key, and you need to ensure that there is not only a good physical building to purchase but also that you will be able to attract the right tenant. Returning to the phrase my old boss once told me, 'Disappointment is the difference between expectation and reality.' Put simply, you need to be realistic about what your leasing options are and how the property can make you a profit.

Mentor tip

Most people are unfamiliar with, and wary of, commercial property, but investors often start with residential and move into commercial because they don't have to deal with the everyday stresses of dealing with tenants and maintenance.

WHAT'S THE STRATEGY?

Adding commercial property to your portfolio can be a great idea, and I have many millions invested in commercial properties, each with different reasons for being in the portfolio. The strategy was always to build up a substantial residential asset base *first* before trying to fit any commercial properties in. For everyone, it's going to be different, and the underlying strategy will be determined by your purchasing power, risk appetite and knowledge of the commercial sector.

Investors are often initially attracted to commercial property because they hear that it has high yields. Commercial property can be an extremely lucrative investment strategy. That's because the tenant pays all the outgoings, and you just collect the rent and pay the mortgage. Sounds easy, right?

If the property becomes vacant, many investors may be forced to accept a lower rent simply because they can't afford to keep the property vacant for an extended period of time. Advanced investors with bigger financial buffers may be able to 'sit and wait' for that ideal tenant. And this is the key point to consider with commercial property: do you have the financial capacity to weather the storm?

With residential property, there are usually some very simple ways to minimise vacancy periods; for example, if you drop your rent by $20 per week, you'll be more likely to secure a tenant relatively quickly (and you'll often have a choice of tenants). You don't want a situation where you only have one applicant for the property and no comparison with another prospective tenant. If the rent is set correctly, you should receive multiple applications and have a choice of tenants. With commercial property, you might need to pay the mortgage for many months (or longer) while you wait for a tenant to show up and check it out.

> **Mentor tip**
> One way to make money using this strategy is to build set rent increases each year into the lease. Common practice is around 3 per cent, but you need to ensure you have a watertight lease prepared by a good lawyer.

WHAT DO YOU NEED TO KNOW FIRST?

The big difference with commercial property as opposed to residential property is that the tenant essentially funds the whole thing for you. They'll typically pay to fit out the premises for their business and then continue paying the rent at a fixed fee. The way to create an increased profit is by building in automatic rent increases each year, usually between 1 and 5 per cent, which means you can literally set and forget and watch the cash roll in. Of course, this needs to be negotiated. Nothing is 'standard', and it will come down to market conditions at the time as to who has the upper hand in negotiations. If the property is vacant and you're struggling to make mortgage payments, you certainly won't have the flexibility to negotiate solid rent increases.

Who wants to buy an asset with no income? No doubt you have seen service stations or fast food outlets advertised as 'fully leased investment with new 5x5x5-year lease'. Properties typically go onto the market when a new lease is signed with a tenant, and the more favorable the terms (to the landlord, such as consumer price index increases and rent reviews), the higher the price.

Basically, when you're buying a leased investment, you're not just buying the property but also the tenant. This gives investors peace of mind that there is a commitment already in place for a fixed period of time, and, if all goes to plan, income will just come in month to month and increase year on year, and hopefully the tenant takes up the option to renew for a further term.

LEASE LENGTHS

Another major difference between residential property and commercial property is the lease lengths. Typically, a residential lease is anywhere from 6 to 12 months, and vacancy rates are typically between 2 and 4 per cent in a healthy market. It's not uncommon for some types of commercial properties to have vacancy rates between 5 and 20 per cent, so securing a good tenant on a good lease is crucial to your success.

When vacancy rates are higher, tenants have more choice, and they also have more negotiating power with landlords. Given that commercial tenants are running a business, they need stability. As such, leases are typically for three to five years, or even more, and there is no cookie-cutter approach for commercial leases. While there are often templates that lawyers will use to draft a commercial lease, everything is up for negotiation – tenants can ask for anything in a lease to make it more appealing to them.

Something a prospective tenant might ask is that the owner (you) contributes to the fit-out of the space, or that you subdivide the space to suit their requirements. They may even ask you to pay some or all the outgoings (such as rates, land tax, owners' corporation or body corporate fees) as part of the lease. Unfortunately, if there are high vacancy rates at the time your property becomes available, you may find yourself having to make a tough choice – lease the property on terms that favour the tenant, or leave it on the market and wait for the right tenant to come along to pay your asking price. It's because of this that you will often see a commercial property in a good location sitting vacant for a year or more.

Commercial tenants are often looking for a home for their business. So, when you're offering your small office on the market for lease, your incoming tenant will need to consider if it is good enough to be the 'home' for their business for the next few years. They'll be thinking, is it a property that I want to bring my clients to? Does it have good access for my staff with public transport, parking and so on? What facilities does it have? These are quite different drivers to residential properties, where prospective tenants are more likely to be interested in things like views, carpets and appliances. Businesses are now looking for extra inclusions to their staff amenities, and 'end of trip facilities' are commonly asked for – these include secure bike storage, lockers, showers and change rooms.

> **Mentor tip**
> When it comes to purchasing commercial property, everything's on the table, from the fit-out to the lease length and rental terms. Let the negotiations begin!

MANY VARIABLES

There are many variables with commercial property, so you really need to be specific with your acquisition strategy to ensure you stack the odds in your favour. For most investors, getting into commercial property seems like a good idea; however, people are often limited in their financial capacity to secure good quality commercial properties. While you can buy commercial property for the same price as an average house in one of our capital cities, lending will determine whether this strategy is appropriate for you.

Lending and finance

As we covered earlier, your financing is critical to your success as a property investor. Lenders don't have the same appetite for commercial property as they do for residential property. Commercial property and commercial lending are more closely linked to the economy and how businesses are performing. For example, when consumer sentiment is high, businesses are optimistic and the economy is growing and doing well, lenders are more comfortable lending for commercial property. But when there is doom and gloom in the outlook for the economy and businesses are suffering, lenders pull back from commercial lending, and it can be quite difficult to secure a loan. This depends, of course, on what type of property you're looking at buying. Often, when the economy isn't rosy and performing well, that's when prime opportunities exist to snap up a bargain – if you have deep enough pockets to ride out the storm.

Assuming you want to buy a small office or retail premises (a shop) in a capital city, you would typically require a 30 per cent deposit, which would give you the most lending options. There are lenders that are comfortable with a 20 per cent deposit, but let's use a 30 per cent deposit for this example. The smaller your deposit, the smaller the pool of lenders you will have access to, which will make it more difficult to secure a good deal on your finance. This means that, with the substantial amount of cash required for some commercial property transactions, it can make sense to purchase a higher-value residential property instead.

Case study

In this example, I have used very basic numbers to show a very simple comparison. Of course, these examples would require the investor to qualify for the loan/s and be able to service the debt, but I think this shows the purchasing power of residential property versus commercial.

Commercial property value: $1 million

70% loan-to-value ratio (LVR)

30% deposit = $300,000

Using that same $300,000 on a 90 per cent LVR would allow you to buy a residential property valued at $3 million. Lenders typically favour residential property because it's easier to sell if something goes wrong, and it's also significantly easier to lease. The reduced risk from a lender's perspective is reflected in the higher LVRs available to borrowers.

Side note – LVR is always listed as a percentage – just to confuse people I guess! LVR is used to determine how much you're borrowing in relation to the value of your investment property. A high LVR means your deposit is small; a low LVR means you have a large deposit and are therefore borrowing less.

Your LVR is basically the reverse of your deposit. If you have an LVR of 90 per cent then your deposit is 10 per cent of the property's value, and you're borrowing the remaining 90 per cent. Understanding LVR helps you compare different finance products and find one that matches your deposit size. Over and above that, it can help you avoid applying for a loan that isn't suitable.

Of course, these are very approximate figures, and there are other factors to consider here, such as your ability to service that level of debt and the much higher stamp duty costs. However, as a guide, banks do see commercial property as a higher risk, hence why there are fewer lenders available and the LVRs are lower.

Lenders know that as the investor, you're likely to need that rental income to pay the mortgage. As such, buying a commercial property that is vacant can cause issues with lending. Many lenders will simply not lend on a vacant commercial property, ruling out a portion of available lenders in the marketplace. Those that do lend on vacant property may require a reduced LVR, which can be as low as 65% (or even less), meaning that even more of your capital needs to be tied up in that investment.

It's also common for lenders to look at your other assets and how leveraged you are. Personal guarantees are usually required for commercial lending, even at low LVRs.

The last thing to consider is that a commercial property being vacant will affect its valuation. A licensed valuer will be sent on behalf of the lender to value the property. Since commercial properties are valued in part on the value of the lease and the terms attached, a vacant property will generally be valued lower than a tenanted one. Add this to the bigger deposits required and commercial property can become significantly less sexy.

What should you buy?

If you're looking for commercial property, as a rule, a bigger tenant means a safer investment. For example, if you owned a commercial property leased to Bunnings, Woolworths, Officeworks, BP or any other tier-one tenant, the risk of tenant default is massively reduced. However, to secure a property like this you're up for many millions of dollars; and, of course, these companies are armed with agents, staff and consultants who will be able to negotiate very hard with you for a good deal.

A good rule of thumb is that the less established the tenant's business is, the higher the risk. The tough part for many investors is balancing the risk of filling the vacancy quickly versus finding a stable, high-quality tenant. On one hand, you need the income; but on the other, having a tenant in your property that can't afford to pay is going to mean inconsistent income, and can result in lengthy legal battles and vacancy periods.

Many people wanting to get into commercial property do not have the borrowing capacity to spend millions of dollars on 'A-grade' commercial property that attracts large and stable businesses, so they end up having to look at more affordable price points. This can often mean buying a 'cheaper' commercial property and having a small business in the property.

According to the Australian Small Business and Family Enterprise Ombudsman, 98.45 per cent of all Australian businesses are deemed 'small businesses', meaning they have a turnover of $10 million or less. More than half of these businesses, however, have a turnover of less than $200,000. Sadly, 60 per cent of small businesses fail within the first three years; so, if you're dipping your toes into commercial property, you need to be aware of these risks.

My recommendation

As with anything new, you must take the time to understand the market in which you're investing. If you want to buy a factory, for example, how many other factories are there in the area? What is the competition like? What sort of tenant will likely lease the property from you? What yield could you achieve? To be completely blunt, you're going to need to spend a lot of time researching not just the area but also the economic drivers and market conditions for the potential tenant. It's significantly more work than with residential property. Not only do you need to understand the basics of property, finance and entity structuring, you need to become a research warrior – researching the competition, knowing what other properties are on the market and speaking to all the local commercial agents, both in sales and leasing, to learn what type of tenant is 'in the market', if any at all. Most investors are limited to a budget of some sort, so that will partly dictate the type of property you can acquire, which could be half the problem. Buying a commercial property that you can afford rather than buying one with solid investment fundamentals is where many investors can go wrong.

Mentor tip

Don't rush into it if you can't afford a quality commercial asset. You're far better off sitting on the sidelines until you can afford it than rushing in and buying a dud that will turn into a money pit.

TOP 3 POSITIVES AND NEGATIVES

Positives

1. Stability: once tenants are in, typically rents come in on time and all other expenses are covered by the tenant.

2. Yields: commercial rents are often higher than residential, and in many cases are cashflow positive.

3. Tenants can often sign longer term leases, typically two to five years (or more), with options to extend longer. This can give the owner peace of mind.

Negatives

1. Businesses can fail, and sometimes a commercial landlord can be caught up in the fallout. This can cause inconsistent cashflow or lost rent for extended periods of time.

2. Vacancy periods can destroy your cashflow. Generally, it's advisable to retain a larger financial buffer as a contingency. As these funds could be deployed elsewhere, there is an opportunity cost in maintaining a bigger financial buffer.

3. Both the sale and leasing of commercial property are linked to external economic factors. Business confidence will affect sale and leasing prices, so you need to be prepared to hold a property and 'weather the storm' if the economy is rocky or business confidence is low.

THE LAST WORD

For most investors, my advice is that fitting a commercial property into your portfolio is something that should only be considered after building a rock-solid residential portfolio first. As with all property investing, building a successful portfolio needs to be done piece by piece, and assets should be added as part of an overall plan and not simply because you 'want' commercial property. Base your decisions on the numbers, your finance capability and your financial buffers, and have clarity on your exit strategy. If it doesn't fit, don't buy it.

***

You've now completed the easy fit strategies – well done! These four strategies are excellent vehicles for you to establish your investment credentials. Understanding how they work will certainly give you the confidence to go out there and try them for yourself. Now, are you ready for your next challenge?

THE
HIGH-RISK
FIT

9

RENOVATIONS

If you've made it this far, congratulations! You've taken lots of information on board and hopefully learnt a thing or two. If Part II was about slowly accelerating, then Part III is about lifting the lid on what's possible at the riskier end of the investment ladder. The next four strategies are all techniques I've used, but they come with more caveats, and you need to proceed with caution. Having said that, they offer fantastic opportunities to build your portfolio, as long as they fit in with your long-term objectives and risk profile.

Your first strategy is renovating. How hard can it be? Grab some cans of paint and some new carpet, block out a few weekends and voila! A reno done and dusted, with huge profits on the way! Reality television shows such as *The Block*, *Renovation Rescue* and *House Rules* present renovating as the bee's-knees way to increase value and make a quick buck – easy, fast and profitable. Other much-loved shows such as *Grand Designs* typically showcase large-scale residential projects, often with quite a luxury specification; after all, that's what attracts the viewers. It's television like this that gets us Aussies obsessed with property – we love it.

I must admit, renovating property is still one of my favorite strategies – for *fun*. That's because I've done the hard yards. I grew up in Perth as a very hands-on kid; I just really enjoyed fixing things.

When I started work in the electronic security industry, I was always on building sites, running cables and using tools. A lot of this was self-taught by watching other tradies and asking questions without having any formal qualifications. Work such as electricals and plumbing were always done by the professionals, though. After all, you can do a 'pretty good job' painting, landscaping or tiling, but there's a lot at risk if you try to do your own electrical and plumbing work. Not only is it dangerous and illegal, but 'pretty good' simply doesn't cut it.

Plus, I was happy to learn some new skills: painting, gardening, working with power tools and basically spending time at Bunnings buying more stuff than I needed to run a job. That's a skill that I have perfected over time – some things never change!

The upshot is that I got to see firsthand how buildings come together, and from what I saw, it didn't seem that complicated. Now, as I look back with the benefit of hindsight, the underlying strategy was that I was renovating older properties as a hobby.

Some investors fall in love with the idea of sinking their teeth into a renovation project. Some want to see fast and easy profits, while others like the idea of having a project to add their own style to.

Renovations really are hobbies for most people who do them. They're something fun to do, where you can get your hands dirty and roll up your sleeves. While a renovation can be a great learning experience, it doesn't directly lead to profits, and I think you need to be aware of this first. Having said that, if it's something that interests you, I would encourage (almost) every property investor to have a crack at it one day. It's great to learn about renovating by doing it rather than talking about it. But the examples of people renovating for a living or making insane profits from a renovation are less common than you might think.

> **Mentor tip**
>
> Always ask your tradespeople for copies of their licenses and insurance cover before they start any work on your property. It's surprising how many unlicensed and uninsured tradespeople are out there. If anything goes wrong, it's likely to fall back onto you. And don't try to do it all yourself!

THE GOOD STUFF

Renovations can be extremely rewarding, especially if you live in the refreshed property and enjoy the fruits of your labour. They're even more rewarding when you have your purpose for doing them – your 'why' – down pat. Generally, there are three camps that renovators fit into, which I covered in my previous book, *Let's Get Real*:

1. Homeowners wishing to upgrade their home: perhaps they like the suburb they live in, or the home has good 'bones' and they believe a cosmetic renovation would make the property more enjoyable to live in

2. Investors who buy a property and 'add value' to on-sell it: they want to either on-sell the property for a higher price or keep it and secure a little extra rent

3. Renovators who love getting their hands dirty and making a property look good: they'll either do up an older period-style home or just rip out the horrible carpet from the 1970s and freshen it up with paint and landscaping.

Personally, I've renovated property for all three reasons, but I haven't always made the best decisions. For example, spending $150,000 on a kitchen renovation wasn't the smartest move, I must admit. However, my intent was to produce a stunning kitchen in the home I live in. When making the decision, it was a conscious move knowing that these funds could easily have been invested elsewhere. The result is a high-quality, well designed and functional kitchen that

I think is cool. It certainly hasn't made me a better cook (nothing can help that!), but maybe if I read the instruction manuals on the appliances one day, I'll be a step closer! You'd be surprised how quick and easy it is to spend 150 big ones on a kitchen; but, of course, that decision was calculated carefully and made using 'play money', not investment money.

Renovating an investment property can be rewarding if you can get in and out quickly to minimise the time the property is off the rental market. Quick cosmetic renovations can attract tenants faster and often produce a slightly higher rental income. Tenants who have a nice, comfortable home that has been freshened up or fully renovated may stay in the property longer and settle in. Conversely, properties that haven't had a tidy-up or a renovation for a long time start to look tired, and tenants may choose to move on to a property they feel more comfortable in.

The best part about renovating as a hobby, though, is that it can be immensely satisfying. Finishing a renovation is fantastic, knowing that all the time, energy and effort spent has produced a great finished product, and standing back and looking at the fruit of your efforts is a great feeling. I have fond memories of going to some of my renovation projects late at night and doing the 'final' final clean before handing the keys over to the agent to lease or sell it. It feels good, like completing a marathon, like my dad used to do many years ago – an amazing effort. Those who have done this will know what I'm talking about: that euphoric (and exhausted) feeling before you collapse in a heap and catch up on much-needed sleep!

THE RISKY BITS

Having said all of that, 99 per cent of the time I finish a renovation swearing never to renovate again! The more experience I get, the more I wonder why I keep doing it to myself. It seems to be a common catchcry among seasoned renovators, too – why do we put ourselves through this pain, time and time again?! It seems there is no end to the blood, sweat and tears involved, despite the overall feeling of satisfaction with the dozen or so renovations I've finished:

- *The blood:* I've had some close calls when renovating, with a few of them causing (luckily) minor cuts and bruises. Typically, this has been on the larger jobs where demolition has been required; for example, knocking down sheds, outhouses, pergolas and other non-structural items. Bathroom renovations are another danger zone, with those sharp tiles and ceramic basins! My tip is always to use protective gear, even though it might be an inconvenience, because I can assure you those products were invented for a reason. I think it would be fair to say that I've copped at least one cut that caused blood on every renovation, even when being careful with protective gear on. There have also been one too many near misses with a crowbar, angle grinder or spider – I HATE spiders.

- *The sweat:* SO much sweat. Renovating is hard work; ignore what you see on television. It might be called 'reality TV', but the reality is that you don't see most of what goes on behind the scenes. There can be a lot of heavy lifting, and rather than listing every body part that will hurt, I'll just say that if you plan on doing much of the work yourself, you're going to be sore on more than one occasion. Lots of sweat, lots of soreness! Of course, you can outsource all the heavy labour, but that's going to increase your costs, which will reduce your profits – which kind of defeats the purpose if you're renovating for profit, but there are many variables to consider. On a larger renovation it may make sense to hire labourers to help.

- *The tears:* At times, you may feel like crying. A lot. Often renovations involve fixing someone else's problem, and many renovators find that they start work only to uncover other problems and issues that need to be resolved. It's not uncommon for renovations to expose bigger problems that need fixing that have been patched up or painted over in the past. For example, you may remove a plaster wall only to find out that there's unsafe wiring, termites or other damage behind it. Often, I see water leaks, which can quite easily be patched up and painted over only to return the next winter, causing you to spend even more money. Sure, it's helpful to find problems then and there rather than having them come back to bite you in the wallet later, but it's not fun. Also, tradespeople, councils and suppliers can all be unreliable, causing unwanted and unexpected delays; neighbours can be problematic; and the cashflow strain can all become just too much for some people. Don't feel bad if you burst into tears (or at least feel like doing so) during a renovation, because I think most renovators get to this point at some stage and, like me, vow to never do it again – until the next one!

With my investor hat on, the blood, sweat and tears are worth it because I don't lose money on my projects. I'm very careful not to overcapitalise, ensuring that the money going into each project is going to give me a return. This means that I don't waste it on home items that are of no value to the property, or that won't increase my yield. So many times, I've seen investors purchase a property to renovate and then waste money on things that don't add any value and are often just their own personal taste, with no benefit to the tenant or new owner. Take a commercial approach to a renovation and do your numbers properly before you buy.

WHAT DO YOU NEED TO KNOW?

A good rule of thumb is to only spend your capital on items that will improve the livability of a property. For example, as an owner-occupier, would you want blinds that block out the light or top-of-the-range luxury fabric imported from Italy? Would you need a fancy $3000 light fitting that looks sexy, or would you be happy instead with a few extra light fittings, or possibly a dimmer switch or smart light globes for 10 per cent of that cost?

The best way to avoid overcapitalising is to focus on a few key areas of the property, and don't (and I mean don't *ever*) get emotionally attached to the property or what you think it will look like when it's finished. As I've said before, treat it like a business, and make business – commercial – decisions only. Use a spreadsheet to do your numbers and track your expenditure. It's the little expenses that creep up and can often add thousands to your total bill. Write yourself a note if you need to:

> 'Luke – at Bunnings, you only need 4 litres of ceiling paint,
> some sandpaper and some masking tape. You do not need
> a new toolbox, a new drill, some new plants, LED lights,
> fertiliser and some new batteries.'

Also, match the renovation to the property. If you have a $2 million house then, of course, the renovation needs to be of a higher standard than that of a $350,000 apartment. Know your purpose for doing the renovation, speak with local real estate agents and property managers to determine the end value and rentability, and discuss your project with them to work out who your target market is. After all, agents are in the market all day, every day (if they are any good), and will have a good understanding of who's more likely to buy or lease your property. Then, engage an independent, third-party advisor to check your numbers. Map out your cashflow forecast and run through it with a trusted advisor, such as your accountant. If the numbers don't stack up, don't do it. It's as simple as that. It's unfortunate that 80 per cent of renovators have a bad experience due to inadequate planning, and this stems from a lack of experience.

Due to my experience, I now approach renovation projects with caution. Why? I've been involved in a dozen renovation projects that

I can remember (some I choose to forget!), and these projects all have two things in common: firstly, they have all taken much longer than they should have, and secondly, they have all cost more money than they should have, despite my best planning efforts. True, renovating a tired old property can be fun, but it does take some effort to ensure that your time and budgeting doesn't get the better of you.

MAKE IT HAPPEN

Having said all of that, renovating is still one of my top strategies because you can make excellent profits. With the right renovation on the right property in the right area, with a proper renovation plan and cashflow forecast, and factoring in all expenses – including holding costs, contingency and selling and leasing costs – overall it can work very well. It's a good strategy for me, but I've been in business for most of my working life and I take a very conservative approach with my investment decisions.

First and foremost, you need to consider the bigger picture. Context. Where is the property? What's around it? What are the fittings, fixtures or, on a larger scale, amenities included as typical for the area? You might want to factor in a reconstituted stone benchtop if this is standard for the location, rather than a cheaper laminate. Or, if the blocks all have landscaped gardens but yours looks like a dog's breakfast, perhaps you might consider a spruce-up.

Mentor tip

Speak to real estate agents in the area to determine if there is even enough uplift in value available to justify the project. If your $50,000 renovation is going to take six months and only add $50,000 in value, then it's probably not worthwhile.

But just changing out the appliances with new ones can make other parts of the property appear older, and that can trigger more repairs and upgrades so they don't look out of place. Maybe you're buying an older property with potential? Do your due diligence, because it could cost you down the track, and remember that the strategy goes hand-in-hand with the property, as we outlined in the previous chapter.

Next, you're going to need the following three key components.

Time

Renovating a property for profit is going to suck time away from you like there's no tomorrow. Never underestimate how long a project is going to take, even if you're outsourcing much of the work. The biggest problem I see when I look at renovations is that they have dragged on – and on, and on. One thing after another has come up, and then the investor finds they've not only lost money by doing the actual work, but they've also lost money because there's no rental income on the property during the renovation.

While outsourcing is a great way to reduce time when renovating, many renovators take on this type of project because they want to be hands-on and do much of the work themselves. Hitting that fine line between doing what you're good at and trying to save money is tough to get right.

One big tip is that when you're calculating your figures, work out how many hours you'll need for the project and allocate an hourly rate to this (noting that much of your work will happen in your personal time, weekends and evenings). Most renovators forget to factor this in, so what might seem like a reasonable profit initially gets stripped back to quite a mediocre return on investment (ROI) after taking in the huge number of hours they need to spend on the project. If you get paid $35 an hour in your job, allocate that amount as a minimum for every hour you will spend on the project. After all, you're investing for a profit, right? If you don't factor this in, you're essentially fudging your own numbers to feel good about your 'profit'.

My top tips:

- Work out how many hours the renovation will take and allocate an hourly rate for the time you will spend on the project.
- Factor in an additional 30 per cent of time for overruns, because you will always underestimate the time.
- Don't be afraid to walk away. Many properties that might look like good renovation projects simply aren't worth touching. Walk away if there's no money in it. Do it. Walk away...

Money

You need money! Even the smallest renovation project or 'tidy-up' job can cost more than you anticipate, as can 'simple' new-carpet-and-paint renovations, because when you do these smaller jobs, other issues pop up. Suddenly, it makes sense to change some light fittings, then maybe do some landscaping, and maybe change the door handles – and while you're there, some of the doors might look a bit mismatched and need to be changed. It never ends, and it's always more than you have budgeted for.

Cashflow can be massively affected without a clear renovation plan. Do all your forecasting upfront before you pick up a hammer. Let me repeat that – get your numbers right before you start *any* work. As I mentioned earlier, you need to match the renovation to the property type and the area it's in. Over and above that, you need to know why you're doing the renovation in the first place – are you selling it afterwards or renting it out?

Whatever your renovation budget, I suggest planning for a minimum of 20 per cent over and above your forecasted costs as a contingency. Professional renovators typically run a project with a 5 per cent contingency, and I have never gone over my 5 per cent contingency on a renovation. However, if you're planning on tackling your first renovation, budget in 20 per cent to be safe. Also, allow for at least 30 per cent extra for time overruns. While there are a lot of variables, this is a good starting guide, especially if you're new to renovating.

My top tips:

- Prepare a renovation plan and detailed budget, and stick to it. These are not to be done on a bit of scrap paper – document them properly and use a spreadsheet as a minimum.
- Save an extra 20 per cent of cash above your costs as a contingency.
- Don't skip cashflow forecasting – do this first! Remember to factor in your buying, holding and selling or leasing costs.

Skills

You need some skills, too. First and foremost, you need to know how to talk to tradies. You need to know the right questions to ask those carrying out the renovation, so you know the signs if you're going to be ripped off. Unfortunately, the only way to do that is to have either worked with tradies before or worked in the building industry. Not all tradies are out to rip you off, mind you – the majority do the right thing and charge for their time and their skills. But, of course, there are always the bad eggs (in any industry!) that give the rest a bad name. At the very least, you should have some idea of how a building works and where the money needs to be spent to maximise your investment and get the biggest bang for your buck. It's important to do things the right way when it comes to renovating, as this is the only way you will make a profit and make the whole exercise worthwhile.

Once you have your cashflow forecast and have mapped out the works that need to take place, you should put together a Gantt chart (see figure 9.1, overleaf) to show what works are starting and when they should be completed. A Gantt chart is a bar chart that illustrates a project schedule. Some trades may need to come in to do a 'rough in' – which means to run pipes, cables and so on, and then a 'fit off', which happens at the end. Some trades make a huge mess, while others are finishing trades that make things look nice, such as painting. If you know all this ahead of schedule and understand the right order to bring in your tradies on your job, you'll save time and money.

Figure 9.1: A Gantt chart

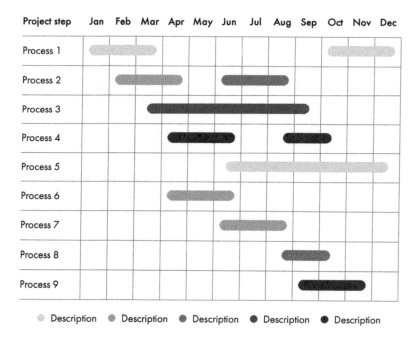

Project step	Jan	Feb	Mar	Apr	May	Jun	Jul	Aug	Sep	Oct	Nov	Dec
Process 1												
Process 2												
Process 3												
Process 4												
Process 5												
Process 6												
Process 7												
Process 8												
Process 9												

● Description   ● Description   ● Description   ● Description   ● Description

One of the biggest frustrations for tradies is when the renovators have no idea what they are doing and rely on their tradies to educate them. Some are willing to assist – 'Call me when the electrician has done his section' – but it's not their job! Trades are ultimately there to run *their* business, not to teach you how to project-manage *your* renovation.

Learning how to talk to tradies is a special skill I've learnt from over 20 years of buying property. While I'm confident now, back at the start I know that many took advantage of my young age and lack of knowledge. The number of times I've had things go wrong where the tradies take no responsibility is far too many to count. It pays to understand who does what, how and why.

> **Mentor tip**
>
> Source your tradies, explain the project to them and get their availability and quote upfront. Ask if there are any likely variables so you're both on the same page from the outset. Never hire a tradie on an hourly rate without having a clear picture of the works agreed to and an estimation of the time to complete the work, or you will likely receive a bit of bill shock.

Lastly, don't try to screw tradies for a cheaper price. They are running a business, and you get what you pay for. Don't offer to pay cash for a good deal. I won't go into the million reasons why, but just keep it clean, do it properly and document everything well. It's better for your tax return and better for the tradie, and it's the right thing to do. If you've done your research, you'll know the approximate costs to get the job done. However, as with anything in life, sometimes the only way to learn is by rolling up your sleeves and getting stuck in. Every renovation is different, and while some tradies have been involved with projects like yours before, some haven't, and some don't ever want to be! Navigating through that can be an experience. If you're lacking knowledge in any of these areas, I suggest you consider some other strategies instead.

My top tips:

- Understand why you're renovating. If it's just a hobby, acknowledge that upfront and don't expect to make a profit. If you do, then it's a bonus.

- If you hate manual labour, dust, dirt, dealing with tradespeople, arranging meetings for quotes, budgeting, paperwork, record keeping and taking on a level of risk, then renovations aren't for you.

- The best way to learn is to have a crack at doing the renovations yourself, but you need to be realistic – don't expect your first few projects to make big profits.

TOP 3 POSITIVES AND NEGATIVES

Positives

1. Renovation projects can be quite rewarding. To finish a project (often after much blood, sweat and tears) is a great experience. Making a profit makes it even more satisfying!

2. Done correctly and with the right planning, renovations can provide an uplift in value to the property without you having to spend a fortune.

3. Much of the work can be outsourced to others, so you don't have to get your hands (or anything else) dirty.

Negatives

1. Time delays in a renovation project can chew up huge chunks of your potential profit. When working on an older property, you never know what problems might arise that need to be resolved.

2. You can't stop halfway! Renovating is a commitment; once you start work on the property it needs to be finished. People often run into trouble when they run out of precious time and money to complete the project.

3. Inexperienced renovators often need to learn on the job, and this often means unnecessary costs and delays that reduce or wipe out profit.

THE LAST WORD

Now what? While renovating may seem easy, there's a lot to consider, as evidenced by the number of tips in this chapter! What I want to leave you with – if you have your heart set on renovating and have identified it as the right fit for you – is the importance of being careful (physically and financially), having fun and trying not to lose sleep over the project. As well as what I've outlined, I'd also advise you to make yourself accountable to someone, whether that's a friend, accountant, mentor or other external advisor. Don't spend any more money than you must (and then only if you absolutely must), and never get emotionally attached to the property. Treat it like a business from start to finish!

10

FLIPPING PROPERTY

Flipping property is another niche property strategy brought into the public eye by reality television. It makes for great watching: a run-down dump is transformed into a stylish, ready-to-live-in home, all in a matter of weeks – or so it seems. The before-and-after reveals are compelling to watch – how did they achieve it all so quickly?!

However, behind the television cameras, the excitement of the journey and the emotional rollercoaster that gets people hooked, there is a *lot* of work done that simply isn't shown on screen. Surely this isn't the *only* way to flip property?

WHAT'S THE STRATEGY?

This strategy is defined as buying a property you wish to sell for a quick profit rather than hold onto for rental income or capital gains. Typically, you buy an undervalued property and then renovate it, adding value, before selling – or 'flipping' – it for more than you paid for it. Who doesn't like the sound of that?

This strategy can be great because, if you crunch the numbers and do your research, you can really turn a profit. Timing is also extremely important with this strategy. To make a profit, you'll need to create a plan and stick to it.

The first part of the plan is to research which areas are selling well, and then narrow it down to a specific property type. Are houses in demand, or apartments?

Once you have identified an area that you're interested in, learn what is selling and how much vendor discounting is happening in the area. Part of your success is going to be buying well, for if you pay too much, you could kill the deal before you even start.

Create a product

The key concept behind flipping property is to 'trade' in and out of various properties. Essentially, when you're flipping property, you're creating a 'product' – or, in other words, a property that will appeal very specifically to a particular market segment.

So, as with any product in the marketplace, you need to have a very good understanding of who your end buyer is, which is a skill on its own. Not only do you need to understand who your end buyer is, you also need to make sure you're creating a product that *lots* of people want, which will give you a choice of buyers at the other end. It's all well and good to create something unique and different, but creating a product that nobody wants or that there is no demand for is setting yourself up for failure. Of course, niche properties do have their place, but they reduce your market for an end buyer and increase risk.

This strategy takes more than simply identifying the right property. It requires extremely careful planning, accurate numbers and proper tax planning. The risks can also be significantly higher than with other strategies because this strategy is often reliant on market conditions over a shorter period. By comparison, many of the other strategies in this book have a longer-term focus.

Investors who wish to flip property must ensure they are aware of the potential ROI to assess if it's worth doing in the first place. Often, I've seen investors with good intentions who have invested huge amounts of time and money into a 'flip' project only to discover that there was little profit in the deal at the end, and sometimes none. They end up breaking even, having a small loss, or end up holding onto a property, waiting for market conditions to improve.

Another thing to look out for is if the area's figures for days on the market have been steadily reducing over the last three to six months, this may show that the availability of stock is tightening. If you haven't bought yet, you may end up paying too much. This is often the case with investors who buy at the wrong time, pay too much and then spend too long carrying out improvements, only to end up with a property that won't give them the returns they were initially after.

This is when flippers become 'keepers'. Investors attempting to flip properties for cashflow inadvertently become 'buy and hold' investors because they overcapitalise, or their timing was off to deliver the right property to the market at the right time. This means they end up holding onto their flip project until market conditions improve, all so they can recover the lost time and money invested in the project. Unfortunately, this happens all too often.

Mentor tip

Make sure your mortgage broker knows and understands what your plans are. Lending conditions change, and if lenders see that you're in the 'business' of flipping property, you may have to change your lending strategy, as traditional residential lending may not be available.

Let's look at four of the most popular examples of what a flip strategy might look like.

1. Renovate and sell

This example is about undertaking smaller renovations that are turned over more quickly. Investors who flip property using this example like to get in and out in a shorter time frame, which means that renovations are typically more cosmetic without a huge amount of structural work. Of course, the investor's business model could be to do smaller and faster renovations or full-scale projects that could take a year or two to complete. But bigger usually means more risk, so my advice would be to start small and go from there.

What you'll need to remember is that usually, the price point you can access for renovating to flip will dictate the size of the project that can be done. To generate a profit, you'll need to act quickly and keep the spend low, because the holding costs can chew up the profits very quickly. Holding costs are the costs that you're responsible for paying while you own the investment property; for example, taxes, insurance, mortgage payments and maintenance.

This is where the art and science of flipping property can take some time to master. It took me a good four to five years and three or more renovations to get into the 'groove'. Knowing how much money to spend will depend on the price point of the property and the expected sale price. Being conservative with your figures is critical because overestimating the sale price gets most people into trouble.

Sticking to cosmetic work, such as painting, landscaping and soft furnishings like carpets and window coverings, is a good rule of thumb.

Mentor tip

If the work requires a circular saw, a heavy-duty drill or any other power tool, or any form of demolition, you might be about to spend too much money!

Advanced investors with higher incomes, bigger buffers and more appetite for risk can take on bigger projects that can be quite lucrative; however, I strongly recommend that you have a solid property portfolio first before attempting a larger-scale renovation project.

2. Adding rooms

This example is exactly how it reads: adding a bedroom, bathroom or other structural addition to add value. Sometimes, a flip project might be as simple as turning a three-bedroom, one-bathroom property into a four-bedroom, two-bathroom property and selling it for a higher price. Adding rooms is a great example of flipping because this may be the only work needed. If the rest of the property is in good condition and doesn't require work, then *this* may be the time to pull out the power tools. (Well, your builder's power tools at least!)

But it can also mean extra work securing approvals and other compliance from local authorities, which can add time to your project. As we all know, time is money! Many examples of structural work require council approval and a licensed builder to construct the work. Anyone who's dealt with their local council for anything building related will know how time-consuming (and soul-destroying!) this can be. Changing the floor plan of a building, usually a free-standing house, may require more than just a building permit for the construction; often, you need town planning approval that must then be advertised. This gives neighbouring property owners the ability to object, which can further delay your plans.

Over and above that, councils may impose all sorts of conditions on your approval, which can throw a big, expensive spanner in the works. Car parking is becoming more of an issue, and councils may even require additional car spaces to be added if you're changing the floor plan. Often, they will require various energy rating reports and may even request modifications to the existing structure over and above what you're looking to do.

Mentor tip

When adding extra rooms, reconfiguring existing rooms or doing some other form of extension, it may make sense in principle, but you need to know your market to ensure your success.

Let's look at an example (see figure 10.1).

Figure 10.1: A floor plan of an older property

This image shows an example of an older property that could be turned into a three-bedroom, one-bathroom property instead of a two-bedroom and dining room plan. The existing living room could be reconfigured by closing off the double doors, creating a three-bedroom home. The current 'dining' room could simply be repurposed to become the living area.

3. Secure planning approval

This example is about securing development approval for further development, often known as 'plans and permits' or getting a development approval – 'DA' in development-speak. It sounds simple: you go and buy a property, get some plans drawn up by a designer or architect, submit them to council, obtain approval and sell the property with the approvals in place to a cashed-up developer for a tidy profit. Simple, right?

Provided you have undertaken significant research into the area you're considering, securing development approval can be a great way to add value, and often without doing any physical work to the property. This is great if you have a social life (not all of us do, however!) and you don't want to spend every minute of your spare time scraping walls, painting, chipping off tiles or digging up gardens, because that's what's involved in some of our other examples.

The huge drawcard of this example is that you can do much of this work over email and phone. That's because you're outsourcing the design and 'paperwork' to someone else, as well as the submission process to the council, so you don't really need to get your hands physically dirty.

This is also a great example because you can lean on the expertise of others to guide you through the process. You don't necessarily need to be an expert on building regulations, environmental reports, energy efficiency reports, drainage and other civil construction, town planning, density requirements and plot ratios, building works… the list goes on. I think you get my point: there is a lot to know and a lot of moving parts to consider. While you don't need to know it all, you do need to know whether the experts you're relying on do (or don't).

At the same time, securing development approval has its own risks. I have used this strategy before and, yes, I've made a profit in the end. Unfortunately, the downside is that often the type of property that you can apply this strategy to is an older one. That's because new properties are typically approved based on the best use of the land.

It also means that when you're getting all this behind-the-scenes work done, you'll likely end up with a few bills for repairs and maintenance, as well as the regular upkeep of the property, tenant vacancies and so forth. You'll need to ensure you have the cashflow to smooth over these bills, over and above the never-ending bills from council and your consultants. Once you start the process, you're committed, and a lot of unexpected expenses can crop up because no two development applications are the same.

Furthermore, keep in mind that while you may think getting a development approval will add value, any developer considering your plans must be able to make a profit from building whatever you design. Personally, I don't want to take on the risk of that not happening and would much prefer a long queue of buyers to compete for the property at the other end. This means that your designs are critical to the success of this strategy.

I've worked with many developers over the years, and I've faced situations where they are preparing a feasibility on a proposed development prior to making an offer, yet the approved plans just don't add up for development. Someone has gone to the trouble of getting plans drawn up and gone through the entire approval process, yet, at the end of the day, the project simply doesn't stack up. Often these plans need to be scrapped and started again to make a development project viable. Ever heard of the saying 'go back to the drawing board'? Well, this term came about because of investors getting crappy plans approved. (Well, we don't know that *for sure*, but it certainly applies in this situation!)

Design something that developers and end buyers don't want and you could lose your dough and a significant amount of time. The most successful investors applying this strategy are often those with a building, design or town-planning background. In fact, the most successful are those with these backgrounds *who are patient*.

Mentor tip

If the designs won't make a builder or a developer any profit, you won't have a buyer, unless you just happen to get lucky and find someone who doesn't know how to do their figures. Don't take your chances assuming that someone will be silly enough to overpay! They are out there, of course, but relying on them to buy your dud 'permit-approved' site is not a great strategy.

4. Rezone

You may not have heard of this example because it's at the more advanced end of the scale. Essentially, it's about changing the zoning of a property and fundamentally changing its use to flip the property. More specifically, it refers to changing the approved zoning of land from rural to residential, or commercial to residential (or vice versa).

There are other options, too, including rezoning residential properties to medical use (close to hospitals, for example) or to obtain higher-density approvals when councils change their planning guidelines.

The benefit of rezoning is that it can give the value of the land a huge uplift and can also allow for a residential subdivision on land that was previously used for farming, or for a commercial property that was previously residential. You can make a profit because changing the 'use of land' to a more suitable purpose typically increases its value. For example, a house near a major hospital on a main road may be approved for medical consulting rooms and could therefore attract a commercial tenant.

It works if you do a *lot* of research and groundwork. This 'boots-on-the-ground' approach means speaking to local councils and having some amazing real estate agents on your side – or, better yet, buying directly from the vendor. As with all property investing, you need to identify who your end buyer or tenant is. In the example above, you might secure a property in a hospital zone and wish to rezone to commercial, or have an exemption granted, depending on what city you're in.

It's worth noting that there is often a cash injection required to comply with the council's requirements, such as installing fire and smoke detection systems or providing additional onsite car spaces, toilet facilities and wheelchair access.

Not only does this example require skill to pull off successfully, it's also not often available to most investors. That's because it's typically reserved for the bigger players in property and competing with them could send you broke trying. There are often deeply entrenched relationships at play here, and when a 'good' site comes up, many agents will contact their networks first before it even goes up for sale. Believe me, I know this to be true because I get calls and emails about 'off-market' opportunities like this every week. Even then, a high percentage of them simply don't stack up financially.

Many of these types of deals are done 'off market', meaning that you may not ever see them on the main property websites. If you do, it might be a sign that the bigger players don't want the property for some reason, so you need to exercise extreme caution. In this category, you're going to be up against more experienced investors, builders and developers, because this type of work is a key strategy for them, and therefore they already have the networks and connections to buy in advance of any formal or official decisions being made.

Other risks include:

- stamp duty and selling costs, including marketing and real estate agent fees, which can kill a deal and take away most (or all) of your profit
- not having other assets to fall back on if it doesn't go to plan – being a higher-risk strategy, there is more variance in possible profits
- not knowing what you will do with the property if you can't flip it in the time frame you expected and for the price you wanted.

The tip here is to practice with some 'dummy' scenarios. Find a property and crunch your numbers on it. Find out your cost of acquisition, planning approvals, engineers and surveyors quotes, landscaping and any internal modifications. Do your numbers to know your costs, then determine if there's enough profit in selling it. More times than not, it won't stack up, and I hate seeing people dive in thinking it's 'easy' and losing time and money in the process only to be disheartened. Of course, this process is an excellent way of learning, and if this is the pathway you wish to pursue then testing your skills on a few practice deals is a great way to start.

WHAT TO DO NEXT

When considering any of the four examples of flipping above, knowledge is power. So, my best advice is to speak to every agent in the area to learn about what the market wants. And yes, I'm suggesting you ring them all. This is what I did – and still do – and it's what's required if you want to be taken seriously. Take the time to buy them a coffee and find out what the end buyers actually want. Markets can change frequently, and demand for the property you're intending to flip may go up or down. Be prepared for either eventuality.

These are some of the right questions to ask:

- What do buyers want? (It's worth repeating this because it's fundamental to your flipping success!)
- How many days has the property sat on the market? (Do your own research to see if the number of days properties are spending on the market is increasing or decreasing, and over what time period. This will vary from location to location and state to state.)
- Tell me about zoning. What opportunities are there for rezoning in your real estate patch?
- How often do 'off-market' opportunities come up? When they do, who do you offer them to?

Mentor tip

Meeting agents is also great way to start building your networks. Just like any other industry, success in property investing can be about who you know. We've talked about 'off market' opportunities, but how do you expect to get a call about the latest property worth considering from your mate down the road if they have no idea who you are?

Do your numbers

As we covered earlier, knowing the cost of acquisition is vital. Can you buy below market value? What are your stamp duty and settlement costs? What is the land tax payable? What about your ongoing holding costs, such as rates and interest payments?

These are good points to consider, but I would much prefer to buy at market value in a good area than to buy slightly below market value in a horrible area. Remember, you need to appeal to the end buyer: the new owner, developer or end tenant. If it's a horrible location, it will still be a horrible location when you've finished flipping.

You can substantially increase the profit at the back end by buying the right site at the front end.

If you do your numbers on your cost base, then add your planning permits, council fees, consultant costs and holding costs together, you can very quickly see a huge chunk of cash evaporate from your bank account. So, you need to have good relationships with your agents to know if you are being fed pie-in-the-sky end sales prices or if they are being realistic. I also advise you to seek a second opinion from someone you trust, and also invest in paid valuations from an independent valuer. Your accountant will be able to run through the numbers with you and ensure you are aware of all your tax obligations, too.

Make commercial decisions, and don't overestimate the profit that might be available. Be realistic. Understand that flipping property is for cashflow only. Remember that long-term wealth is accumulated by building an asset base, and by selling the asset, you can never make money from it again. Make sure you understand how this strategy will fit into your long-term plan and how this will affect your borrowing power.

TOP 3 POSITIVES AND NEGATIVES

Positives

1. Buying a property and adding value to flip for a profit can be quite lucrative with the right amount of research, timing and good luck. Knowing which areas to research and how to narrow down which property to buy is critical for success.

2. Flipping property can be a fast way to increase cashflow and can assist you to move on to bigger projects.

3. If the timing of the market is right, you can use that to ride the wave of price increases if you can identify who your end buyer is and add value that someone will be willing to pay for.

Negatives

1. More people lose money than make money by attempting to flip properties because the costs add up quickly, and markets can change throughout the duration of the project.

2. Entry and exit costs to do this strategy are high, with stamp duty, holding costs and selling costs payable over and above any other costs. In addition, the taxes on profits can be huge because the asset is to be sold.

3. This is a cashflow strategy, not a long-term asset-building strategy. Understanding this is important because buying and selling property might bring in some extra income but doesn't help to build an asset base for long-term wealth.

THE LAST WORD

If you have done your research, you should know what you will be able to flip the property for and how much profit is in the deal. Keep in mind though that the whole process, including planning approvals, can take anywhere from six months to three years (or more), depending on the site and, of course, the elusive town planners in council.

So, you need to be able to weather the storm. The property market in that area may be performing well when you buy, but when you go to sell again it may not be as buoyant. On the flipside, it could have increased substantially. Understand that you need to take the good with the bad on this one – some you win, some you may not. Typically, this strategy is suited to investors who have other assets and financial buffers to fall back on should this strategy not go to plan.

11

PROPERTY DEVELOPMENT

'I want to be a property developer!' After mentoring hundreds of people over the years and discussing the goals of thousands of investors, it still amazes me how often I hear that. Why is it that so many people want to be property developers?

Property developers drive great cars, wear nice clothes and drink coffee all day having meetings – don't they? They make millions of dollars a year 'putting deals together' and cruise around visiting their developments. Stress free, carefree and living the pinnacle of a property investor's dream life. True? Maybe.

I believe property development is an excellent property strategy, which is why I've included it here. And in my opinion, there is an excellent opportunity to make huge amounts of money by being a property developer. However, it probably won't look like the above – at least in the beginning.

THE 'ART' OF DEVELOPING

Essentially, the 'art' of property development involves buying land, financing real estate deals and building and orchestrating the process of a development from start to finish.

The general unwritten rule is that you'll need a 20 per cent margin, which is your profit. Anything less than that is higher risk. That means if you create a $10 million property development, you'll pocket $2 million. But you'll need to factor in expenses such as holding costs, understand when to spend and when to save, and set up the right entity and tax structure to ensure that your profit is the most tax-efficient it can be.

Property development – running development projects, handling various planning and building matters, doing research and due diligence, sales and marketing, and managing millions of dollars – takes a very specific skillset. It's not a career path that you want to learn 'on the job' given the quantum of money that is involved. The huge risks associated with a project that fails can quite literally ruin your life and set you back decades, or in some cases bankrupt you. In creating real estate, developers often take great risks, too – but the rewards are equally as great, which is why it's so popular.

Mentor tip

Be open to what type of developments you want to do.
Many developers are out there hunting for a specific type of development. Keeping your options open gives you the ability to assess the numbers on different projects and potentially profit from something that you may not have considered previously.

Importantly, property development is not the same as property investing. The developers who are building projects year in and year out have a completely different approach to me and you as property investors, whose intention is to build long-term, sustainable wealth. They are a world away, and the skillset required is vastly different. Yes, property is the common denominator, however that's where the similarities end. The difference between doing a one-off, small-scale subdivision as an investor and a small unit development as a property developer is that the latter is a full-time role. Doing one or two small-scale projects does not, in reality, make a property developer. I did a few paintings many years ago, but that certainly doesn't make me an artist or a professional painter. The difference is the experience and having a portfolio of properties you've completed.

MOVING PARTS

When it comes to property development, there are a lot of moving parts. Let's start with the broader economy – the big-picture stuff. Is development in your area supported at a council, state and federal level? Most of the time the answer is yes, because developments are typically good for jobs. However, at council level there may be an anti-development stance. Even at a micro-level, if there's an existing development already in place in the street you want to develop in, your development may get sent to a tribunal for further clarification.

The thing is that all these factors are out of your control, and this grey area can increase risk. You may never know some of the issues, either – they take place behind the scenes – so you need to be prepared for the unpredictable extra time that property developments can take up.

Another way of looking at this is to simply accept that things will go wrong. Build in your contingencies and make a proper plan, and you'll be well placed to ride out the bumps. I like to advise a contingency of 10 per cent of your project value as a good buffer. Of course, this can be reduced over time as your skills increase, but to begin with you will want to have a good chunk of available cash handy – there's every possibility you will need it.

WHAT YOU NEED

This is the basic process for property development:

1. Do your due diligence and research on the area in which you're planning to build.

2. Organise your finance and funding solutions, not only to purchase the land but also to secure development funding to do the project. (Most people are going to have to borrow money to do a development; buying the land is often the easy bit.)

3. Gather your expert team, comprising good legal and accounting professionals (which means you're going to need to know what questions to ask and how to structure yourself properly).

4. Plan your sales and marketing. How are you going to sell the development? Is there a market for your development? Can you sell the properties? How quickly can you sell them? What if you don't sell them for the price you expect?

Cashflow

The most successful property developers have access to good asset backing and cashflows *first*. This means not relying on the development itself to fund day-to-day expenses and being prepared to inject your own funds into the process. The most successful don't rely on the development project to put food on the table on a week-to-week basis and can weather the storms that are inevitable with any development project.

If you become a developer without having enough assets and cash behind you, you will most likely either fail to reach your property development goals or, even worse, you'll be sent broke. I've seen this time and time again, and it's not pretty. I know a guy who keeps trying to become a developer but has failed so many times. Not only that, he's sold down most of his assets to keep his dream of being a developer alive. Now, in his early 50s, he's still a long way off and will struggle to make up for lost time. Over and above that, he now has very little in assets to fall back on.

What's important to understand is the way that property development works – and again, it's all about cashflow. Yes, you can do a development and 'keep' some of the stock, however you will find that a successful property development business separates the cash-flow component from the asset-accumulation goals of the owner.

Risk assessment

Like any investment, your next step is to assess risk. Yes, there is a lot of money to be made in property development, but the risk ultimately comes down to the individual, so you should weigh up the following before entertaining the thought of becoming a property developer:

- What is your appetite for risk?
- Do you have a solid asset base to fall back on if the development project fails?
- Do you have access to (lots of) extra capital if the project requires a cashflow injection?
- What skills do you have in research and due diligence, planning and building, sales and marketing, construction management and commercial funding?
- Have you ever run a business before and managed cashflows?
- What happens if this project fails altogether, and how will that affect you and your family personally?

As I mentioned at the start of this chapter, a property developer takes on significant risk and is often the last to get paid. If you don't want to be stressed and on edge, losing sleep every night, then that risk needs to be managed in advance before you launch into a development career.

One of the biggest risks in property development is delays, which can occur at any stage of a project. These cost time, and we all know that time is money. This is even more apparent when you're holding a multi-million-dollar piece of land that continues to cost you in interest repayments, land tax and council rates, for example, all because you are waiting on pre-sales, waiting for council to sign off on something, waiting on the bank to approve a finance facility or waiting on a builder or other contractor to perform their duties.

When these (usually unavoidable) delays happen, successful developers will be able to sit in a holding pattern until they can progress the project to the next level. That's because they've got cashflow, and it often means dumping more and more cash into the project to keep it afloat. When I explain this to people, they say to me, 'Well surely you can plan for this, right?' Yes, you can plan for delays to an extent; however, some of the developments I have been involved with personally have still gone over time due to external factors beyond my control.

What you need to remember is that this is considered 'normal' with property development. And even planning for the worst-case scenario can still present you with problems that you hadn't considered!

The risk really comes down to your planning, skills and access to funding, and the team involved in the development project. You see, there *are* developers out there all day, every day, making great money from property developments. These are the property developers who have established businesses that operate with hard facts and figures that make good business sense. At the same time, there are also developers out there who *lose* money all day, every day. Often, these losses could have been prevented with proper planning, the right team and the right buffers in place, but quite often their losses are due to external factors.

At the end of the day, property development is a cashflow strategy, as I outlined. Most successful developers build and sell their stock, make their money and move on to their next project. Typically, property developers are developing property to sell to generate income as a business, not to keep a few properties on the side – while this is the perception of how developers build wealth, most of the time this is not the case.

Drop the ego

You've got to know when to drop your ego and listen to your advisors. For a lot of people, emotion is what gets them into property. It was for me many years ago. Swanning around in a Lamborghini, breezing into the site for a quick check and driving off for a latte is what I imagined life would be like for a developer. But if your ego is driving all – or even some – of your decisions, you're getting into it for the wrong reasons, and you'll end up coming unstuck.

Instead, you must take the emotion out and make commercial decisions based on facts and numbers. You've got to be willing and able to listen to advice, and as I've said before, treat developing as a business and have a commercial approach. How well do you run your own personal and household finances? When was the last time you felt financial pressure in the past five years? You must be comfortable with pressure and understand that when things get tight, you need contingencies in place.

Don't talk yourself into a development project for your ego's sake. Moving from wanting to be a successful developer to actually being one requires keeping your ego in check and knowing when to proceed with a project or walk away. Believe me, there is no worse pressure to have in your life than financial pressure – it's horrible, as many of us have unfortunately experienced at one point or another.

YOUR FIRST DEVELOPMENT

If you don't have assets or cash, the best way to step into the development world is by starting small with a backyard subdivision or a small unit development. Know the process, but at the same time, don't expect to make a lot of money.

From a high-level perspective, the concept of a small-scale subdivision is quite simple: typically it involves a residential block of land that you subdivide into two or three blocks to build on. When considering a small-scale subdivision, you not only need plenty of patience and access to extra cash, but you also need to know how to navigate your way through the maze of skills required to successfully deliver the project and still make a profit.

As you'll read in my case study below, a small-scale subdivision can either make or break you. 'Small scale' can often mean 'bigger risk' – when you're looking at a small project, you have less potential profit that can be made and therefore less tolerance for things to go wrong.

Case study

My property on Scott Street in Seaford was a great learning curve: a 'simple' backyard subdivision. The initial plan was to renovate the front house while sorting out plans and permits through council to build a single-storey unit in the backyard. This simple concept made sense at a high level, but drilling into the nitty gritty is where developments like this can run into trouble. As you might expect, the success of any development is in the details.

My initial conversations with the council and reviewing of planning requirements indicated that a two- to three-bedroom home could be built on the site, but of course this was always subject to the specific design and no guarantees are ever made by councils. After purchasing the property, I quickly got to work on the planning application and engaged a local building designer who I'd worked with previously. A few iterations of designs were prepared, and ultimately the plans were submitted to the council for approval. The time frame for council to assess the plans blew out and, close to six months and a few design changes later, I had approval to build a two-bedroom, two-bathroom, single-level home.

Renovating the front house, I spent countless hours working in my spare time: painting, demolishing, landscaping and cleaning to get it ready to lease out. When the planning permit was finally issued, I then had to select the builder for the rear home. This is where things got interesting, because some builders specialise in this type of work and some don't. I learnt the hard way navigating through who did and who simply wanted a build to keep them busy in between other projects. Small build jobs like this are often more hassle than they are worth for many builders, and subsequently the build quotes varied dramatically.

When the project was finally finished, the whole process had taken just under three years. While I did make some money in increased equity (because I didn't sell), the time it took was certainly time I couldn't get back. There were many lessons, however I realised in hindsight that unless you have the time, money and patience (and some good sleeping pills), those smaller developments can be inherently riskier because there is quite often less profit in them, meaning that delays or unexpected expenses can cost you in both time and money. You need to consider the opportunity cost also, with your funds tied up for three years in a small development when they could have been deployed elsewhere and made more money for you without the risk.

FINDING LAND

Sourcing the right piece of land is crucial: not all land is created equal. A lot of people wrongly assume that the size of the block is the most important thing. That is important; however, it's not what you *can* do with it that counts but what you're *permitted* to do with it!

Size is an important consideration when it comes to blocks of land, and each council has different requirements and guidelines. Thus, having a 'big block' doesn't guarantee you will get better results. Furthermore, planning guidelines change from time to time, too, so you need to know what you're buying over and above the piece of dirt. What was once zoned for rural 20 years ago may be zoned rural/residential or even plain residential now. In 20 years' time, land that is zoned industrial may be rezoned into commercial, residential or mixed use as our population increases and our cities need to find better use for the available land.

For example, you may have a 5000-square-metre parcel of land in a great location, but if only part of that land is viable for development then it may not stack up. Site costs can add huge additional costs to your development project and can often make your small-scale subdivision project completely unviable. However, in some cases, site costs can add value to the land as it may give you alternative aspects and views that were unavailable previously – but, of course, this extra cash injection must be recoverable from higher sale prices. You need to be very careful with this to ensure you don't overcapitalise, just like with renovations.

TREAT IT LIKE A BUSINESS

The next most important part of property development is securing funds. An important rule of thumb here is that if you're building fewer than three townhouses, you'll typically be able to apply for residential lending. Anything over that, you're looking at commercial lending, and this is quite a different process: the banks will scrutinise your figures to within an inch of their lives, and yours, and if you don't know what you're doing or how to present your figures properly then they'll simply throw it out.

As I've said before – and I'll say it till I'm blue in the face – to be taken seriously, you need to treat investing like a business. Remember Mr Moy, from the introduction? *Repetition is boring.* And that means presenting the figures in a professional business plan. The lenders are making a commercial decision, so you need to present a business plan so that they can see your skills and experience as well as your figures. Part of the lender's due diligence will include doing a credit check on you as the director – they will review anything and everything, and the Australian Taxation Office and Australian Securities and Investments Commission have a lot of information available. They can see if you have any credit defaults, whether you have been bankrupt and if you have had a company liquidated, among many other interesting things. From a high level, what they're asking themselves is, 'Does this deal make sense for us?' If you have a scrappy little spreadsheet and no real explanation for how you're going to sell the properties, it won't reflect well. How are you going to sell them? What research have you done to support those prices? The bank wants to see a full pack and the whole deal, not just a spreadsheet of numbers. They also want the whole lot in one go, not in dribs and drabs – if your application is 'all over the shop', it's likely going to be a 'no' from them.

Here's a list of some of the items you'll need to include:

- 100 points of ID for each applicant (typically driver's license and passport)
- details of the borrowing entity (name, address, Australian Business Number, Australian Company Number and directors' names)
- an organisational chart detailing the ownership and relationship between entities
- a copy of the title
- a copy of the planning permit/regulatory decision/letters of extension
- a copy of the endorsed plans
- details of any current finance for the project (including funder, amount and status)
- the contract for the purchase of the land
- contracts for any pre-sales and evidence of deposits
- the sales price list

- the marketing agent's profile, marketing proposal and agency agreement
- the builder's profile
- the building contract
- the valuation
- the quantity surveyor's report
- the geotechnical and environmental report
- a statement of assets and liabilities for the borrower and guarantors
- the last two years' financials for the borrowing entity
- proof of funds for the balance of the project
- a copy of any trust deeds (if applicable)
- feasibility for the project
- a developer profile.

You can see that it's quite a list.

THE RIGHT STRUCTURE

Work out how much money you have and what you can afford. Then, speak to your expert team to sort out the structure you're going to need. The most common structures are under a company or a trust, or a combination of the two. If you're going to be a developer, you'll also need to set up what's called a special purpose vehicle (SPV). In most cases, this is a company and trust structure to do the development, but you will need this before you go on and sign any contracts.

EVERYTHING ELSE

When it comes to small-scale subdivisions, you must factor in the following points as a minimum:

- initial purchase cost of land
- stamp duty

- legal fees
- demolition
- pest control
- surveyor's costs
- engineering reports
- environmental surveys/reports
- town planning/council fees
- bank fees
- interest costs
- agents' commissions
- marketing fees.

THE RIGHT PRICE

Right now, most small development projects in any capital city in Australia are going to include a land component of between $500,000 and $2 million. Yes, there could be the odd project outside this range that is considered 'small scale' to some people; for example, if you buy in a suburb that already has a median house price of over $2 million, you could build three townhouses and consider it a small-scale project. But generally, when you spend more than $2 million acquiring the land, you're moving into a different ball game altogether. On the flipside, it's possible find a backyard subdivision for less than $500,000, but we're talking about average figures here as a guide. Most small-scale subdivisions are going to fall in the range of $500,000 to $2 million, which is the space that 80 per cent of small-scale developers operate in.

There are also many people offering joint venture (JV) opportunities or profit-shares in development projects. Make sure you fully understand what you're getting into and how your capital is protected before you give up your hard-earned capital to a third party. Higher returns do not mean a better investment – I would much rather a lower return in a safer investment than to put my capital in something offering huge double digit returns that never eventuate. I've seen property companies come and go over the years offering 20 per cent, 30 per cent or even up to 50 per cent returns. I've had conversations with our members who tell me how lucrative the returns are with XYZ Company and that they wish to place their money in those investments. While some might work and investors do get the returns offered, it's very rare; and, to be blunt, if they need to offer those types of returns to attract people's attention in the first place, there must be a good reason for it!

BEATING THE COMPETITION

When buying in the $500,000 to $2 million price point, you need to consider your competition. Who are you competing with to buy those parcels of land for your small project? I'll tell you this much: it's not the big players. The large-scale corporate developers typically steer clear of small subdivision projects because their eyes are on the bigger profits. The actual process itself is very much the same whether you develop three townhouses or 30. If 80 per cent of buyers are competing for properties under $2 million, then that also means it's the most competitive end of the development spectrum.

Some of your key competitors in this price bracket are actually builders. Yes, local builders between jobs often want to keep their staff and contractors employed, so they may do a small subdivision to keep the doors open or for a bit of a boost to their cashflow. This might not seem like a big problem, but consider this next point: when you're doing a small-scale project, no doubt you need to hire a builder to build the properties. You have your initial costs of land acquisition, then you need to pay the builder to build your new dwellings, and then, to make a profit, you need to add a premium on top of all of that. The builder will make a profit already on the build job; as a result, they can pay more for the same land you want to buy because they don't need the development margin you do. Their motivations for doing the project in the first place are different to yours, too, and if you're forced to spend more, that'll cut into your potential profit, which increases your risk. I've seen this time and time again: people end up paying ridiculous amounts of money for land and convince themselves it's a viable project.

Builders can impact your ability to acquire land in a few ways:

- The builder can often afford to pay a higher price on the initial land cost as they are just looking to make their build margin.

- The builder may know the local market better than you and thus know when to stop when negotiating on price.

- The builder does not necessarily need to make a development profit over and above their build margin. They treat it as just another build job, as they are more interested in maintaining their business cashflow than becoming millionaires by doing these projects.

- Some builders actually do this full time and buy 'off market', so you may never even get to see the 'good' sites as they never hit the market.

Now, of course, there are plenty of builders out there who know how to get their build job and a development margin; they would be silly not to. But this is what you're going to be up against in your bid to acquire land in the most competitive price brackets. And if you can't get the first part of the process right – buying the land – you might be put off moving to the next part.

UNDERSTAND YOUR MARKET

A lot of people will treat their backyard subdivision like a renovation and overcapitalise by putting things into the build that they shouldn't. For example, spending money on stone benchtops, top-of-the-line appliances, landscaping, high ceilings or aggregate driveways may look good and only cost an extra 10 to 20 per cent, but that eats into your profit, and your profit will disappear if you keep spending when the area doesn't demand it.

Instead, speak to real estate agents in the suburb to get their opinions. You might want to build a nice two-storey luxury home, but the market only calls for a tiny little three-bedroom, one-bathroom shoebox because that's what people want. As I mentioned Chapter 10, getting the product right is critical to your success and can make or break the project.

It's worth keeping in mind that subdivisions can be just as hard as doing ten or 20 townhouses because you're fitting your house into an area that's already got a house behind it, plus a house next to it on either side, and then you've got a front house, too. So, you're trying to squeeze something in that must fit in with ever-changing council requirements around parking, environmental impacts, overshadowing, setbacks and a raft of other things that can make it more difficult.

BUILDING

At this point, once you have engaged them, signed contracts and paid your deposit, most commercial builders undertaking multiple builds will be capable enough to look after everything without involving you. They'll just want to formalise colour selections and other key design aspects prior to getting on site, as part of the contract. Then, it's through each of the different stages of construction that you will get involved. If you're building a house or a townhouse, the stages are as follows:

1. Deposit/contract execution
2. Slab stage
3. Frame stage
4. Fixing stage

5. Lock-up stage

6. Completion.

On completion, you will conduct a final inspection, and it pays to have an expert building inspector go through the build, too. I recommend finding someone who specialises in new builds and is completely independent. Then, it's a matter of working through the defects and resolving them with the builder. On any new build, there is always something wrong; typically, even with the best builder you will still find small defects, and most builders are happy to return and rectify them once notified. I have found, however, that there can be minor defects that builders do not cover, so sometimes it's easier to just suck it up and fix things yourself, as frustrating as it might be. You just have to be pragmatic.

Lastly, make sure you're tracking your figures every step of the way and ensuring that you know exactly what's flowing in and out of your accounts. Even if you have a fixed-price contract, you'll still need to be across your insurances, cashflow and any other costs that go above and beyond the build.

> **Mentor tip**
> Reinvest your profits. If you successfully pull off a development project, pay all your tax and other expenses, and you're left with a profit, the temptation is there to take your profits and buy a new Tesla, right? Well, maybe not a Tesla specifically, but the point is that taking your profits out and spending them rather than reinvesting them will only slow you down.

TOP 3 POSITIVES AND NEGATIVES

Positives

1. Yes, it's possible to make money in property development – a *lot* of money. Of course, this must be balanced with your tolerance

for risk and ability to secure the 'essential ingredients' for a successful development.

2. Successful developers can often build substantial brand equity over time, building on their past successes. This can help with things like site acquisition, securing finance and end sales.

3. Experience builds experience. You can learn from a 'textbook' or by paying someone $30,000 to teach you, but there's nothing like experiencing property development firsthand. It'll equip you with skills and knowledge to help you tackle your next project if you get bitten by the bug!

Negatives

1. It looks a lot easier than it is. Buy a piece of land, get some drawings approved, build, sell and you're a millionaire, right? But for every success story you see or hear about, there are 99 other developers who have failed, and failed big time. There are so many things that must go right, and if you fail, it can send you broke.

2. You win some, you lose some. If you have substantial financial buffers and a good asset base, then go for it, but be prepared to lose some – or all – of your capital. Your ability to weather the storm can make or break your project. External factors can easily affect your project, despite your best efforts – it's happened to me and can be heartbreaking to put in all that time, energy and effort only to watch your profits reduce by the day.

3. Knowing where to go for funding, how to fund your development, how to present your application, what terms to sign up for and how to not get ripped off are all minefields that trip up developers. It's little surprise many end up having to juggle their finances just to ensure their project stays afloat.

THE LAST WORD

As we mentioned before, whether big or small, property development is tricky to get right unless you know what you're doing. So is skydiving! But if you've decided that you're ready and willing to kickstart your development career, you should embark on these projects to learn the process, not just make money. One of the biggest mistakes I see is when people become emotionally attached to their first development project and don't take a commercial approach to their decisions. I know I have mentioned this before, but it's such an important point to make. Having said that, it's human nature to be more emotional when starting something for the first time – I know I was – but do your best not to convince yourself that you have a ripper project when you actually have a dud.

There are developers out there running very successful businesses and making millions of dollars each year, but there are also developers failing miserably. Remember that development is typically a cashflow strategy and not an asset-accumulation strategy. With 99.9 per cent of investors just needing to build their asset base, property development can and should be something done by those with the financial resources to do so and enough assets to fall back on in the worst-case scenario. Plan, and have a contingency and a good team around you. If you do decide to pursue property development, make sure it fits in with your long-term plan and that you have factored in time delays, additional capital requirements and possibly even loss of capital.

12

SHORT-STAY ACCOMMODATION

Most of us are familiar with this type of property; most likely we've all either stayed in an Airbnb ourselves or know someone who has. The main reason that this strategy is popular over a long-term rental strategy is that the returns can be higher.

You might have an Airbnb or short-stay property for a year or two and then switch it off. For many people, it's not something they have to take that seriously because they're only doing it for a bit of extra pocket money. People like to 'give this one a go' and see how it works. Your mate is doing it on a property in South Yarra, a sought-after suburb in Melbourne, but you've got a place in Berwick, further out of the city. Why not give it a go, you ask?

The reality is that you must manage guests and furniture. You must learn how to price – and how to tweak your pricing – along with everything else that goes with managing a listing. And most people are self-taught if they're treating it as a hobby.

What we're talking about in this chapter is investing for the long-term and using this property strategy to increase your yields so you can increase your servicing on loans, borrowing capacity or debt servicing, depending on what tactic you're going to use to allow you to buy more property. So, again, it's about how this strategy fits into your overall portfolio plan.

You should be approaching this strategy in the same manner as all the others in this book: like a business. That means taking a strategic approach when it comes to all the things you'll need to be across:

- the supply and demand fundamentals for the area and for the actual property itself
- the check-in and check-out process – how is that going to work, and who will do it?
- pricing to account for long weekends and holidays, and competing with hotels and motels
- smaller details such as wi-fi passwords, broken taps, and smoke alarms beeping and upsetting guests.

Mentor tip

You need a lot of time to make this a strategy play, which is why many who offer Airbnb properties use it as a side gig and genuinely love and are proud of the hospitality service element. Either you use your time, or you pay someone to manage it for you.

AIRBNB

Is Airbnb just a short-term craze or a global giant here to stay? Well, no-one can deny that Airbnb has disrupted the hotel industry and short-stay accommodation market ever since it launched in 2008. The issue more recently is that COVID-19 has decimated profits for the entire short-stay industry and many property owners who used this strategy – so much so that many investors have flipped over to the long-term rental market in high-density areas as they are no longer able to capitalise on tourists. But the hospitality juggernaut has served millions of new guests year on year and spread to many countries all over the world. Most Australians have now stayed in an Airbnb, and for many it has become the preferred option for holiday accommodation over a hotel room or serviced apartment.

As a result, consumers are voting with their wallets, and the business is certainly not slowing down any time soon. And that means there are opportunities here for investors to increase their yields and rental returns. However, the global pandemic did put the brakes on travel; some investors built their entire portfolios on short-stay properties, and many have gone into panic mode trying to restructure their finances and portfolios.

The strategy

One of your first considerations if you're considering Airbnb to increase rental returns is to assess your appetite for risk. One of the biggest risks involved in this strategy is fluctuations in cashflow. One month you may have a very high occupancy rate, and the next month you may not have many bookings at all. Therefore, balancing your books and managing your cashflow is critical – you need to ensure you don't drain your account every month.

Two key rules:

1. Have enough of a financial buffer to get you through periods where bookings are low.

2. Aim to double your baseline rent when setting your price, considering your effort, energy and effort, as well as opportunity cost. For example, if you can get $400 per week on the long-term rental market, you should aim to average $800 per week on the short-stay market to make it worthwhile.

If you decide you're comfortable with the cashflow risk, your next step is to identify and investigate your property. Is there market demand for it? Areas in market demand will likely be within walking distance of a CBD, business park, café or restaurant strip, public transport or other sporting or entertainment facilities. These are more likely to be in high demand throughout the year, while some areas may only be in demand seasonally. For example, beachside towns may be extremely popular during the warmer months but struggle to attract bookings during winter. Make sure the property isn't reliant on one thing – if it's near a popular tourist attraction which then closes, that will likely affect your yields.

Your best bet to determine the competition is to do a quick search on Airbnb, which will show other properties in the target area, if any. Some property types and suburbs are simply not in high demand, and while you may believe you have the best property in the area – and maybe you do – that doesn't mean it would make a great Airbnb property.

Property presentation

Assuming you're comfortable with the cashflow risk and your property is in an area that will have sufficient demand, you next need to determine how to present your property to the market in its best light.

Your green shag pile rug and family photos on the wall may make *you* feel warm and fuzzy, but they're not impressing anyone else. Sorry about that! Instead, look around and review your property through your guests' eyes. If it's already furnished, you may need to declutter and make the place feel comfortable – but don't make it too personal. If you have an empty property, this gives you an opportunity to style and fit out the property to suit the market you're targeting. Are you targeting families or young professionals?

Decorate to suit your target market, but also be mindful that you want your property to appeal to as many people as possible, so a more conservative approach will appeal to a wider market and increase your chance of attracting more quests. People are typically looking for a more homely stay than a hotel – something with a little more warmth. However, there's a fine balance that you need to strike between giving your guests the warm and fuzzies and not making it too personal. At the same time, it needs to be clean and tidy but not too clinical with no personality. Your personal taste may not appeal to others, so it's best to ask your friends, family and trusted advisors what *they* want to see in a short-stay property when they are travelling.

The listing

How many times have you jumped online and glossed over the listings that have crappy photos where the images are fuzzy, or purely of the surrounding area and not the property itself? Don't be that host. Get professional photos taken – spend some money and show your guests that you're taking this seriously. Don't take them yourself or have them done by your friend who's a budding photographer; pay the money, because a good property photographer will be able to tell a story through your property's images, and this takes considerable skill and styling. It's worth it.

You'll also need to write an engaging description, covering in detail what's included in the property. Are you offering a room, or the entire house? It's better to be specific than risk a bad property review, which will translate to fewer bookings, because the reviews are a vital part of a guest's decision process. Savvy hosts create a 'brand' for their property and play on specific themes or details, complemented by images that support the narrative. For example, a house may be marketed as highly sustainable and green, with its recycled materials or passive design; or it might have beautiful period details and be on a single level, which may appeal to older guests who don't want stairs.

Finally, the price: don't set it too high. It's better to start with a lower price and test the market. See how you go with bookings and adjust your price accordingly – even if you feel your property is worth a higher price. As I mentioned before, Airbnb guests rely heavily on reviews, so you will want to attract people to get your first bookings.

If you're the 'new listing on the block', you may only be able to compete on price at first – even if you have a stellar location and fancy furniture! It can take a good 12 months to get the pricing right for your property, as there will likely be variables that you haven't considered and seasonal changes that require regular price adjustments.

> **Mentor tip**
> Presenting a property for a guest is not about you, it's about them. Every decision made must be tailored to the needs of your guests.

ROOMING HOUSES

A rooming house is typically a house with many bedrooms that is split into multiple separate rentals. Instead of collecting rent from one property, rent is collected from each individual tenant. A four-bedroom house may have four different tenants, for example, but it could also be a three-bedroom house or even a ten-bedroom house. A good way to think about this one is that it's like a 'share house' but with strangers: four completely different tenants who don't know each other living together and sharing the accommodation.

Generally, investors who apply this strategy are looking for a higher yield on their property, which means they're looking to charge a higher level of rent across the property. And overall, rooming houses can be a successful strategy. However, there are a few 'buts'. Yes, you may achieve a higher rental return on the property, but this is a very risky strategy offset with a lot of compliance, additional management costs and, generally, higher costs for maintenance.

The strategy

To make a rooming house work, typically you'll need a minimum of three bedrooms. However, some rooming houses can have eight to ten (or even more) rooms, and they will still work effectively. It's worth understanding that rooming houses do not work in all areas and often (but not always) attract lower socio-economic tenants, mainly due to affordability. I'm a big believer that there are good tenants everywhere, and regardless of someone's background or circumstances in life, everyone should be given a chance, however it takes a special skill to get the right mix of tenants in the property.

With effectively strangers in the house, you'll need to consider the social implications of this strategy more so than with a simple, one-rental property. Will your tenants all pay their rent on time? Will they get along? The chances are that if you're renting out rooms in a rooming house to tenants who don't know each other, they may not see eye to eye.

What to consider

When considering if a rooming house is good for you, you'll need to factor in the view of the lender, who will treat rooming houses differently to a standard residential property. Required loan-to-value ratios can be as low as 60 or 70 per cent, which means you will need to put significantly more cash into the deal to get your finance over the line.

On top of this, there are layers of compliance to be met (as I referred to earlier), all of which will incur extra costs. Some considerations include:

- increased security (such as door locks on each room)
- furniture, such as living room furniture and kitchen appliances
- extra fire protection, such as smoke detectors in each room, fire extinguishers, and regular checking and auditing of fire protection provided
- exit lights and emergency lighting
- storage for tenants
- additional parking requirements
- significantly increased property management costs

- increased insurance costs
- permits required from the council and other authorities
- a reduced pool of lenders for financing the property.

All this – along with the extra costs and upfront cash involved in providing and maintaining the facility for your tenants, and the higher turnover of tenants – needs to be weighed up against the slightly higher rental return. When using this strategy, investors chasing cashflow are often disappointed when the expected returns don't eventuate, and I have had many people look purely at the returns without factoring in the sheer amount of work involved. Now, I'm not here to talk you out of this strategy, but there is no fast-track to wealth, so make sure you pay attention to the good, the bad and the ugly before diving into this as an investment strategy. Does this fit your risk profile and your property plan?

Mentor tip

There can be a lot of trial and error (often more error than trial), and because this is such a niche investment option, you need to be extra careful. Even if you find a property manager to take this on for you, you will still likely be heavily involved in managing the property.

MAKING SHORT-STAY ACCOMMODATION WORK

To make these strategies work, there are a few things that will need to work in your favour. Firstly, you must be extremely selective about the property you choose. For example, you might buy a property in a high-rise tower with amazing views, and it looks great in isolation, but you didn't do any research on the area; soon enough there's another tower being built next door blocking the view that was the only thing that sold the property to guests in the first place. You'll have a property looking into another building instead, and you'll have to drop your price.

Think about how you like to travel. You want to ensure your property has:

- Plenty of natural light, so that guests don't feel as if they are living in a shoebox. When it's dark, you don't want the lack of light to affect your rent or nightly rates.
- A great location that's close to amenities. Think of the reasons why people travel: in most cases it's to be close to a business district, which then also needs to be close to cafés, bars and restaurants, because if they're travelling for business they're going to want to go out for dinner.
- Excellent maintenance. Your cashflow will go up and down like a yo-yo with all the bits and pieces you'll need to fix or be across to meet guests' expectations. Guests expect much more than tenants, so you need to be ready to meet their requests and needs – and get used to long days.
- An external cleaning company. Take it from me: if you lease the bedlinen and towels instead of buying them, you'll never look back. Cleaners will come in, rip everything off and take it away, saving you a huge chunk of time.

PROPERTY MANAGEMENT

While guests breeze in and out of their short-stay rental, there's a lot of work going on behind the scenes. Hosts must manage check in and check out, as well as following up guest feedback (good and bad) and coordinating cleaners and other maintenance items. This can be quite time-consuming if you're managing it all yourself. After all, you're providing accommodation services akin to a hotel, so it's no wonder guests expect high levels of service from their host when they're used to receiving excellent service from other hosts and from hotel chains. The bar has been set pretty high, so you need to be 'on your game' all the time.

What's important to note is that there are now professional companies that specialise in Airbnb management. These companies are experts in analysing cashflows, occupancy rates, pricing strategy, cleaning services and, of course, guest services. If you're serious about using Airbnb to increase yields on your investment property, you can mitigate the risks involved by using a professional management company to manage all of this for you.

While the initial fees may appear high, remember they are dealing with scores of 'tenants' (guests) for your property every year. They're dealing with every issue, such as the wi-fi not working, toilet paper running out and cleaners not turning up, which means time saved by you not having to deal with this. As a result, they do a lot more work than a traditional property manager with a single tenant on a 12-month lease.

As with other 'hands-on' property strategies, make sure you have factored your own time into your figures. If you're going to spend an extra ten hours a week doing this, what is that time worth to you? What is your hourly rate? Deduct that from your expected return and your true profit is the difference between that and the long-term rental yield.

THE BANKS

To make this strategy work, the banks or any lender will wish to see consistent income over two years. So, if you're getting $1000 one month, then $3000 the next, then $500 and then $2000, the banks aren't going to use that income to assist with your servicing. Banks want to see stability, as anyone who's self-employed would know.

If you're applying for a loan, they will look at your last two years' tax returns and average out your income. If it's up and down, they'll smooth it out and spit out an average. Of course, you don't look at the property the same way. You might have a few good months over Christmas and Easter, but most months you're not hitting that consistent income, and often the banks will want to see two years' history on that property. So, from a lending perspective, short-stay properties can trip you up or slow you down, because it's the inconsistency that the banks don't like.

If you're going to use short-stay accommodation to build your portfolio thinking you're getting a higher yield and be able to borrow more money, it might take you two years of good income, similar to being self-employed. That's two years of *good income*, not just two years of tax returns. This means spending two years building your Airbnb business, getting the reviews in, increasing your prices and building up the financials so you can borrow more money. Put simply, you need to take it seriously and not just 'give it a go'. There are several banks or vendors that won't accept Airbnb income, so you need to be aware of who will look at you from a lending perspective.

TOP 3 POSITIVES AND NEGATIVES

Positives

1. Higher yield can put more money in the bank each week, even after all expenses. Many investors have built a great cashflow portfolio this way.

2. You may be able to use the property for your own holidays – who doesn't want a property by the beach they can use for a few weeks a year! Providing you disclose this personal use in your tax return, it can make owning a holiday home more affordable.

3. You control your income to an extent. If you wish to be more conservative, you don't need to charge a premium; so, if consistency of income is the most important factor, you set your prices accordingly. You may also take a more aggressive approach and charge a higher fee but take less bookings.

Negatives

1. Guests can cause damage to your property, which can cause huge headaches. Trying to fix damage with only hours before another guest checks in can be quite challenging!

2. Insurance can be expensive, hard to get and hard to claim. Make sure you do your research into your insurance options before taking on this strategy. Read the policy in detail before signing up because there can be many hidden exclusions.

3. Getting finance can be difficult. Ensure you can keep borrowing if you're planning on building your portfolio or this strategy could actually slow you down.

THE LAST WORD

This can be an amazing strategy to increase yields. Who doesn't want to watch the money roll in week after week? But, as with all our strategies, you'll need to weigh up the time involved in doing it yourself versus engaging an external professional company to manage the entire process for you. As one of my favorite sayings goes, 'Just because you can, doesn't mean you should!'

CONCLUSION –
WHERE TO NOW?

Congratulations! You've made it through my eight property strategies to best fit your 'why'. If you know your 'why', treat investing like a business and have the right fit, there's no stopping your potential!

For me, successful investing is about the long-term and not making a quick buck. I've set up the best systems and processes for me to follow and finetune the right property to fit into my portfolio.

Of course, as you've read, this hasn't happened overnight. It never does, despite what you read! There are no overnight successes. My success has evolved over many years and continues to do so. After working with so many people over the years and seeing what goes wrong, this book was written to teach you that while a lot of so called 'fast-track to wealth' strategies are available, there really is no fast-track to wealth or silver bullet out there that will do all the work for you.

The fundamentals of long-term property investing work, and always will. Yes, investing does carry some level of risk, as I've outlined across Parts II and III, but this risk can be mitigated with the right education, the right team of people around you and an informed and educated plan of attack.

To sum up:

- You need to fit each property into your portfolio to match your long-term goals.

- Know your 'dreams, dates and dollars', and work backwards from that end goal.

- Understand that your goals will change over time, and that's normal and OK. As your knowledge and education improves, with each purchase you'll become a better investor.

- Slow and steady wins the race. It's worked for me, and I'll continue investing forever because, like any skill, there's always more to learn. There are always more people with big goals for me to help.

When you start out with any of these strategies, and even when you make your very first property purchase, you're initially what is often called 'unconsciously incompetent'. But over time, your knowledge increases, and you realise how far you have come; and then you realise that you're 'consciously incompetent' (see figure 13.1). Not that you're incompetent as such, but there's a point where you have an 'aha' moment and realise you actually didn't know what you were doing.

Figure 13.1: Becoming unconsciously competent

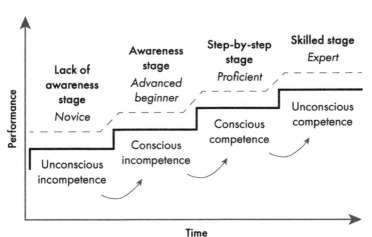

With more time and more education, as you get better at what you're doing, you become 'consciously competent', and then the final stage is when you become completely comfortable with your abilities – 'unconsciously competent'. This is something I like to refer to, helping me acknowledge the journey with all of its failures and successes. It's when you wake up one day and say, 'Hey, look at how far I've come – wow, I actually know what I'm doing!' Once you've achieved the expert level of unconscious competence, ensure you continue to practise and develop your skills and knowledge to attain ongoing world class mastery, and don't become complacent!

Throughout my journey, I've been through all of these stages at different points, and it's understanding them that has helped me to educate and inspire other property investors.

Often, you don't even need to buy dozens of properties – you may only need a single property or two to achieve your goals. But whatever you do, make sure it's the right fit. I find it sad seeing people 'try' property investing, only to give up because they took advice from friends and family, the media or a salesperson who didn't have a deep understanding of what they're trying to achieve. They buy the wrong property at the wrong time for the wrong price, with the wrong strategy and the wrong advisors around them.

If only they had the right ingredients for successful investing in the first place; they could have had an entirely different outcome! That's me and my team's mission at The Property Mentors – we genuinely care about our members' long-term success.

The fun part? Well, you'll never know it all (although there are plenty of investors out there who are know-it-alls!), because there's always more to learn and experience. The property market will always have its challenges with interest rates, governments, tenants, building issues, compliance and changes to tax rules. However, the fundamentals are still there. If you have the right *property fit*, you can achieve the life you desire. It may not happen overnight, so you'll need to be patient.

Delayed gratification is an incredibly frustrating thing for us property investors, but believe me, it's all worth it. I couldn't imagine my life any other way, and I have had the benefit of helping so many people over the years. We are all on our own journeys, and we all have different goals and dreams. Nobody can take that away from you, so don't let go of the things that are important – do whatever it takes to achieve your goals. You're only on this planet once, so give it your best!

At the end of the day, you've done brilliantly to get to the end of this book, and I congratulate you for taking the time to explore your property fit. Investing in property is actually simple, but it's not easy. And the best thing you can do after finishing this book is to get started. Do something, make it happen, because unfortunately nobody is going to do it for you. As I said in the introduction, you can always make money, but you can't get the time back.

As I mentioned earlier in the book, we have *incredible* opportunities to build wealth in this country – we really are lucky. But those opportunities slip by each and every day, with most people unaware of what they could be doing if only they got out of their comfort zones and took some action.

Having said that, I do live in the real world; and I know that, as the poet Robert Burns wrote, 'The best laid plans of mice and men often go awry,' – meaning your long-term plans can and will change, just as the property markets will. There's only so much planning you can do, but essentially, true mentoring is about having someone to lean on and share the good times and the not so good, the moments of success and the moments of fear. As a successful investor, you get better at navigating and adapting over time – as long as you don't give up.

One of my favorite quotes is by Steve Jobs:

> *'You can't connect the dots looking forward; you can only connect them looking backward. So you have to trust that*

the dots will somehow connect in your future. You have to
trust in something – your gut, destiny, life, karma, whatever.
This approach has never let me down, and it has made all
the difference in my life.'

So, while there are a lot of technical things to consider when investing for the long term, there's also your gut feeling, your trust, and your desire to live your ideal life – that burning desire that won't go away. Stick with it.

I'd like to end the book with something my dad shared with me a few years ago. It may seem unrelated to property, but bear with me. In fact, it's a powerful story that's stayed with me ever since, and I think about it often whenever I'm feeling at a crossroads.

It inspires me to take a big-picture view and reassess what's important, to slow down a little and 'get real' about how I live my life. All of the goal-setting, risk, due diligence, finance applications, stress, uncertainty and market conditions can get a bit much at times. Property investing is not a solo sport; I need to rely on my team of advisors, just like you. They have helped put me back on course and focus on the long-term goals. But despite setting new and bigger goals year on year, this story that Dad shared with me will always bring me back to earth and remind me what is important in life. It's a paraphrased version of a parable called 'The Businessman and the Fisherman', which is thought to have been originally written by Heinrich Theodor Böll. I'd like to share it with you here:

> An American businessman was at the pier of a small coastal village in Mexico when a small boat with just one fisherman docked. Inside the small boat were several large fish. The American complimented the Mexican on the quality of his fish and asked how long it took to catch them.
>
> The Mexican replied, 'only a little while'. The American then asked why he didn't stay out longer and catch more fish.

The Mexican said he had enough to support his family's immediate needs. The American then asked, 'But what do you do with the rest of your time?'

The Mexican fisherman said, 'I sleep late, fish a little, play with my children, take siestas with my wife, Maria, and stroll into the village each evening where I sip wine and play guitar with my amigos. I have a full and busy life.'

The American scoffed, 'I'm a successful businessman and could help you. If you spent more time fishing, you could use the proceeds to buy a bigger boat. With the proceeds from the bigger boat, you could buy several boats; eventually you would have a fleet of fishing boats. Instead of selling your catch to a middleman, you could sell directly to the processor, eventually opening your own cannery. You would control the product, processing and distribution. Of course, you would need to leave this small coastal fishing village and move to Mexico City, then eventually New York City, where you would run your expanding enterprise. In 15 to 20 years, when the time is right, you would announce an IPO, sell your company stock to the public and make millions!'

'Millions,' the Mexican said. 'Then what?'

The American said, 'Then you would retire and move to a small coastal fishing village, where you would sleep late, fish a little, play with your kids, take siestas with your wife and stroll to the village in the evenings, where you could sip wine and play your guitar with your amigos.'

Don't wait. There's never going to be a perfect time, so get started NOW.

To your success – *adios amigos!*

INDEX

PRAISE FROM MEMBERS AND PARTNERS
OF THE PROPERTY MENTORS

I started working with Luke over fifteen years ago, originally providing accounting services to one of his very early business ventures. We share a passion for property, and it's been a pleasure watching as Luke goes from strength to strength, growing an amazing portfolio of his own. Likewise, it's really satisfying working with Luke and the team at The Property Mentors. Luke is as passionate as I am about making sure each and every member of The Property Mentors has the very best structures in place, optimal asset protection, and that they are receiving the right advice and assistance to achieve their own uniquely individual plans for the short, medium and long term.

Mario Vinaccia, Veale Accounting Group, Melbourne

As a newly single woman, I suddenly found myself in a position where I needed to ensure my future financial path was going to not only be manageable for me but able to provide me with the results I would need into the future. The Property Mentors were a great support, clearly laying out the steps required to reach my financial and property ownership goals.

Kylie, 48, Sydney

I was a 19-year-old keen on property investing but had no previous guidance in what to do or where to start. After working with The Property Mentors, I've been able to secure two properties at the age of 23, with plans for many more to come.

Cody, 23, Melbourne

I was eager to invest and plan for my future, but I was uncertain which investment avenue I wanted to take. I found myself jumping between various investing ideas, but I was scared to take the initial step and actually invest. The Property Mentors helped me focus on, and flesh out, my personal and investment goals. They helped provide clarity and a framework for me to start investing and building my property portfolio.

Joshua, 29, Sydney

I was in a rush to invest but unsure exactly what to do. After beginning work with The Property Mentors, I realised that the missing piece of the puzzle was that I needed a mentor who was also an investor to help me! The Property Mentors allowed me to create a portfolio faster than I could have imagined, and now I can see that I will actually be able to achieve long-term financial freedom.

Weliner, Adelaide

Ever since I was about 18, I had developed a mature interest into gaining an investment property. I didn't know how I wanted to go about it and didn't have a full grasp as to what it could actually do for me financially, I just wanted to put my money into a safe investment. Fast-forward four years and both Bree and I had signed up for a membership with The Property Mentors, and within the space of 18 months were able to secure our third property.

Chayse, 24, and Bree, 22, Queensland

I was an owner of one investment property and wanted to purchase further properties, but I wasn't sure how to go about it. The Property Mentors have a lot of experience and knowledge to share when it comes to creating a long-term strategy and determining how and when a property may suit this goal.

Joanna, 30, Canberra

While I had limited savings, I really wanted to get into the property market. The team at The Property Mentors helped me access an opportunity that I wouldn't have been able to find on my own, allowing me to get into the property game and start my investment journey earlier than I ever dreamed!

Tin, 23, Melbourne

I came on board with The Property Mentors at the end of 2018. I wanted to do something with my cash other than having it just sit in a bank account or spending it on a new car. I had no property at the time and was researching my options. After talking with a few different people, I kept in touch with The Property Mentors and I ended up joining their program. Becoming a member has actually saved me money by stopping me from making mistakes which would otherwise have cost me a whole lot more! Joining up also provided me with confidence and motivation. My ultimate goal is to replace my salary to live comfortably by the age of 35, and I'm well on my way now!

Riley, 26, South Australia

We have been fortunate to have been guided by The Property Mentors, who have patiently supported us through the bumps and hiccups. Novice investors like us would have been wiped off the market – let alone having the property portfolio we have now – without following their lead. We are so grateful for their help.

Kaz and Greg, Sydney

I bought my first investment property without a great deal of clarity about what my goals were and how I would achieve them. A short time later, I came across The Property Mentors, and it was refreshing to hear about their one-on-one approach, to engage in valuable online and offline sessions, and to feel a part of their community.

I've been afforded some great opportunities through The Property Mentors and, with their support, I'm making good headway with my investment goals, and am feeling confident about next steps and comfortable making decisions around my financial future. I can't recommend Luke and the team at The Property Mentors enough!

Lisa, Farley, New South Wales

Prior to coming on board with The Property Mentors, we had our primary place of residence and one investment property. We'd been trying to get into our next investment property, but just had a general lack of knowledge about how to best do it. We were also struggling to find the right properties to fit our needs. Now, we've purchased an investment property in Melbourne, we've got the ball rolling and we're looking at next steps. It's nice to know that there are always options no matter your circumstances, and that we now have a team to help us with our goals.

Helen and Neil, 40s, Penrith, New South Wales

Property investment seemed like an interesting option, but I hadn't done any research and was naive about the market and the methods involved in growing a portfolio. Luke was down to earth, with no BS, and together we quickly sorted out my goals, established my situation and got to work. Now, I'm living in my new home on an acre in Tallai, and using my previous home as a weekender. I've purchased an apartment in Ivanhoe, a commercial property in Geelong, a townhouse in Cannonvale and another two blocks of land in Airlie Beach, with houses to come. I have absolutely no regrets, and Luke and the team have 100 per cent of my trust!

Phil, 65, Tallai, Queensland

We have been members of The Property Mentors for three years now. In that time, Luke and his team have helped build our property portfolio from zero to three properties, and counting. All of our interactions with The Property Mentors leave us feeling inspired and excited for our property investment journey and what's to come. Our only regret in our journey is that we didn't find them sooner!

Bec and Leigh, Woori Yallock, Victoria

I had money to invest and wanted to invest wisely, and property seemed like a good option. I knew that I didn't know enough about property to do it all on my own, so I started investigating my options. Luckily, I came across Luke's first book – *Let's Get Real*. I attended one of his workshops in Brisbane, and the rest is history. With the help of the team at The Property Mentors, I now realise that there are plenty of ways to make money through property investment.

Daniel, 35, Brisbane

Before working with The Property Mentors, I'd saved a deposit, but it was just sitting there not earning anything. I'd spent many hours trying to learn what I could on my own so I could make the best property decision – all while running a business! The additional burden of doing my own research was just adding increasingly to my limited time and causing extra worry. I definitely had what they call 'analysis paralysis'. The Property Mentors helped me to take a step back and not be in such a rush, so I could focus on my business while letting other people with more knowledge provide the support and guidance for property purchases and negotiate better opportunities.

Cindy, 55

major st
PUBLISHING

We hope you enjoy reading this book. We'd love you to post a review on social media or your favourite bookseller site. Please include the hashtag #majorstreetpublishing.

Major Street Publishing specialises in business, leadership, personal finance and motivational non-fiction books. If you'd like to receive regular updates about new Major Street books, email info@majorstreet.com.au and ask to be added to our mailing list.

Visit majorstreet.com.au to find out more about our books (print, audio and ebooks) and authors, read reviews and find links to our Your Next Read podcast.

We'd love you to follow us on social media.

in linkedin.com/company/major-street-publishing

f facebook.com/MajorStreetPublishing

instagram.com/majorstreetpublishing

@MajorStreetPub